"Offers the perfect antidote [to] unsatisfactory work culture. We're [told] work has to be something we try to escape, but Zigmond shows us how to bring Buddhist principles into the art of work and make it a joyful and relaxing part of your life."

—Ginny Hogan, comedian and author
of *Toxic Femininity in the Workplace*

"This small book is packed with insights, practices, wisdom, and humor, all guaranteed to make you the most popular bodhisattva at the water cooler."

—Eddie Stern, author of *One Simple Thing:
A New Look at the Science of Yoga and
How It Can Transform Your Life*

"A refreshingly practical guide. . . .
Zigmond brings a light touch to meaty content."

—Randy Komisar, venture capitalist, entrepreneur,
author of *The Monk and the Riddle*

"Can you actually find happiness and fulfillment
and even 'wake up' at work? *Buddha's Office* provides
readers with a path to help you do just that. Warm, funny,
and packed with practical wisdom, this book by
Dan Zigmond might just change your life."

—Amy Sandler, CMO and Coach at Radical Candor

Buddha's Office

Buddha's Office

The Ancient Art of Waking Up While Working Well

DAN ZIGMOND

RUNNING PRESS

PHILADELPHIA

Contents

PART 3: HINDRANCES

PART 4: PERFECTIONS

INTRODUCTION

Waking Up at Work

BUDDHA NEVER WORKED A DAY IN HIS LIFE. HE WAS BORN about 2,500 years ago, grew up a pampered prince in ancient India, left those riches behind to become a wandering monk, and ended his life as a revered spiritual teacher—all without ever earning a salary.* It's not clear that he ever even handled money, and he forbade his closest followers from doing so.

So why would anyone want to know what a freeloader like that had to say about work?

Let's start by backing up a bit. A few people today still follow the Buddha's literal example and renounce worldly possessions, living their lives as full-time monastics. In fact, probably more do than you think—estimates range from a few hundred thousand to a million or more worldwide. But if you're reading this book, I'll bet you're not one of them. You have not chosen to spend your life cloistered in a temple or monastery, let alone wandering the rural countryside of some far-off land without a fixed address. Neither have I. For better or worse, most of us today do not live as Buddha and

---

* And it's not that he was busy doing a lot of housework, either. He left home the day after his only son was born. It's safe to assume that he did not change any diapers before he left.

his core disciples did. One way or the other, most of us spend much of our adult lives working.

Some of us basically hate it. It's a rare treat these days to find anyone who truly loves their work. Too many are working long hours at jobs they can't stand. The lucky ones look forward to the weekend, when they can have two days of their *real* life back. But many in high-stress careers don't even do that, grinding through their Saturdays and Sundays, barely slowing their pace, charging toward some hoped-for early retirement or other future reward. Most Americans don't even take all the vacation they're allowed.[1]

Those lucky few who do love their jobs often have their own frustrations. Maybe it's nonstop stress or lack of resources or miserable behavior by colleagues or clients. Or maybe work is fine, but you just wish there was a little *less* of it. It seems that everyone with a demanding career laments their work-life balance. Does anyone *really* enjoy answering emails and texts at all hours? And all of us who are racing and striving like this may be in for a surprise. A study in 2016 found that work-related stress was the fifth largest cause of the death in the United States.[2] Some may not make it to retirement at all. (More on this in chapter 2.)

It doesn't have to be this way. And Buddha knew this, 2,500 years ago, without ever setting foot in an office.

When Buddha had his great awakening—when he literally became *the* Buddha, which means the Awakened One—he listed "right livelihood" among the eight keys to an enlightened life. He knew somehow that work was important, and that working *right* was essential. As he traveled through ancient India, spreading the word about his newfound path of spiritual liberation, he preached not only to other wandering monks like himself (and eventually nuns), but also to those he called "householders," who he encouraged to follow his teachings while remaining in the workaday world. Even two-plus millennia ago, Buddha understood that most of us would spend much of our waking lives working, and would have to find our enlightenment there.

Buddha was raised among the privileged 1 percent of his day and became an honored guest of kings and queens, but he was also surrounded by subsistence farmers, artisans, and small-scale merchants who struggled to survive. The Buddhist scriptures, usually called the sutras, refer to dozens of professions already practiced in Buddha's time, and his audiences included everyone from royalty to slaves.[3] For most people hearing the Buddha's words, work was a necessary and central part of their daily lives. He couldn't ignore it then, any more than we can ignore it now. Enlightenment was not something just for full-time monastics, so Buddha knew that helping ordinary people work right was essential to helping them find their own path of awakening.

That's what this book is about: how to make our work not just another distraction, but an integral part of truly waking up.

This book will help you understand why Buddha—a guy who never held a job—chose to elevate *right livelihood* to such importance. More importantly, we'll explore how to find a way of working that's "right" in every sense of that word: right for you, right for your health, right for your sanity, and right for the world.

Buddha's teachings are not complicated. He laid them all out in his very first sermon in about 700 words—about as many as you've already read in this book so far! Most of them come down to basic principles, like honesty and balance, that help us pay closer attention to the world. But applying those simple teachings to the complexities of daily life can be quite a bit trickier. As Buddha elaborated on these concepts over the years, his teachings ballooned to about 20,000–80,000 pages, depending on who's counting.

Despite his complete lack of job experience, Buddha actually had a lot to say about work in all those later sermons. Some of his admonitions were both specific and unsurprising. (He suggested that we avoid careers in weapons, human trafficking, and drugs, for example.) But once you start pulling on even those simple threads, it's easy to unravel the whole sweater. When Buddha says to avoid business in "intoxicants" and "poison," what does he really mean? I spent years working at Instagram and Facebook. Are those online platforms intoxicants? Are they even poison? I suppose some people would say so, although I disagree. Should we consider television an intoxicant? What about video games? Are coal miners trafficking in poison? Or car manufacturers? Some people talk about sugar as a poison—so are ice cream shops forbidden? That's a depressing thought.

In any case, these specific suggestions are just the beginning. All the same principles Buddha offered to guide us in the rest of life must also guide us in our work. After right livelihood, the other seven elements of the eightfold path are right view, right resolve, right speech, right conduct, right effort, right mindfulness, and right concentration. All of these can help us at work—especially mindfulness and concentration, which we'll spend extra time discussing. Most of us know from sad experience that there are endless ways to stray from this path in the workplace—to fall into *wrong* conduct, *wrong* speech, and so forth; to treat our coworkers badly; to drift mindlessly from one task to the next; even to lie, cheat, or steal. We'll talk about all these things, too, and how to avoid them.

Buddha taught that life involves a lot of suffering, which many in the working world will find very easy to believe. But he also taught that it doesn't have to, that suffering has a cause and a cure. That cure isn't necessarily *easy*, but it is *possible*. And it's just as possible behind a desk or at a cash register or in a factory as it is on a distant mountaintop.

You don't have to quit your job to find enlightenment. It might not even help. Buddha's life was kind of an American dream in reverse: starting in the lap of luxury and ending literally penniless.* He found all the bliss-chasing of his youth to be a distraction. As nice as retirement might sound right now, it isn't any easier to wake up on a beach or on a golf course or at a spa. Buddha would tell you it might be harder.

You don't have to become a Buddhist, either. Buddha never used that word, and might not be thrilled with the way people use it today. He didn't believe in "Buddhism" per se—he believed in paying attention, taking care of yourself, and waking up. That's something anyone of any faith can do.

In the end, happiness and fulfillment at work depend on many of the same things that bring us happiness and fulfillment elsewhere. Like anything worth doing, there are no shortcuts. There's no pill you can take or magic notebook you can buy or fancy exercise you can learn. But this book will show you how Buddha's simple instructions apply to our everyday lives in the office or on any job. Before long, you'll find yourself waking up while working well.

---

* The wife and son he abandoned were eventually ordained and joined Buddha's burgeoning community of monks and nuns, so his one and only descendant ended up broke, too.

PART I:

INSIGHTS

CHAPTER 1

Why Work?

SHORTLY AFTER BUDDHA'S ENLIGHTENMENT, TWO TRAV-eling merchants named Tapussa and Bhallika were passing through a neighboring village. It's not entirely clear how word had already gotten around, but one of their local relatives mentioned to them that a holy man nearby had recently become what he called "wholly awakened."[1] Even in ancient India, where wandering mystics were a lot more common than they are today, this was a big deal. The two men gathered some food to bring as an offering and went off to find this Awakened One. The story goes that they caught Buddha a little off guard. He hadn't started teaching yet—he hadn't even decided to become a teacher—and he didn't have a bowl handy to accept their gifts of barley and sweets. But he found something he could use and the two were so impressed by his mere presence that they immediately converted and became his first disciples. Then they continued on their way.

So the very first Buddhists were two ordinary people on a business trip.[2] (Keep this in mind the next time you're killing time in an airport or stranded at a Holiday Inn.) Many years later, when recounting a list of his foremost disciples,

Buddha still remembered their names and mentioned them first among all the laymen he had taught.[3] Think about that: Before there were any monks or nuns shaving their heads and donning saffron robes, there were these guys—two regular Joes, going about their daily lives, trying to earn a decent living, yet eager for a glimpse of something more.

Two thousand five hundred years later, the world is still full of Tapussas and Bhallikas—spiritual seekers with a day job. And I'll bet you're one of them.

Many of us wonder why we have to work at all. Wouldn't it be easier to find ourselves, to find our own enlightenment, if we didn't have to? Surely a trust fund would help.

To be clear, this is not a new problem. We've been working for a long time. And I don't just mean you and me—I mean all of us, all of humanity. For as long as people have lived together in anything resembling a human society, we've had to work.

Buddha understood this and accepted it. In fact, he was much more likely to get the opposite question: Why *stop* working? In a famous lecture, a local king asked Buddha exactly this. The king's servants and staff—everyone from elephant riders to weavers, soldiers to bath attendants—produced useful things. Through their labors, the king explained, "They bring happiness and joy to themselves, they bring happiness and joy to their mothers and fathers, to their wives and children, and to their friends and acquaintances."[4] Compared to all that, what good was Buddha's hours and hours of sitting around?

Buddha explained to the king the fruits of meditation and spiritual life, and we'll talk about that later in this book, too. But for now my point is that Buddha didn't have to explain the fruits of *working* life. Those seemed obvious to everyone. He had to defend *not* working.

As both that ancient king and Buddha understood, there are lots of good reasons to work. For some of us, our jobs feel like a calling. Maybe you've wanted to be a doctor or a lawyer or a firefighter or a nurse or a teacher for as long as you can remember. Or maybe you discovered such a passion later in life. Maybe you've found some way to turn your love of art or sports or music into a job that pays your salary, and so you work mostly because you simply love doing what you do.

For others, work is a mission. You see a problem in the world and feel duty-bound to solve it. The day-to-day work itself may not be particularly exciting, but you believe in what you're doing and you feel that you're making a real difference. That is enough.

Other people work simply to earn a living. Whether you're supporting a family or supporting yourself, there's absolutely nothing wrong with that. Beyond the lucky few born into riches (like Buddha) or those who choose to live by the generosity of others (also like Buddha!), we all need a way of paying the bills. And that's great! It feels good to be financially responsible and independent.

For most of us, work is probably a mix of all these things.

Often, it changes over time. When I left college, I thought I might become a traditional Buddhist monk and live out my life in a remote temple in Asia. And I did live in a temple in Thailand for a few months, and later in another in San Francisco. But then I fell in love and got married, and ended up needing a job. When I first started working, it was to earn a living and support my new family. I counted the days until I thought I could afford to quit and move on to something more satisfying—literally counted, with spreadsheets and calendars and complicated formulas. Then, over time, I realized that I liked my work, and one day, about 10 years into my career in technology, I decided I didn't want to do something else. I stopped counting the days and focused on how I could do my work better. Now, more recently, I'm focused on the difference my work makes to the wider world, and on helping others find satisfaction and fulfillment in the work they do.

The business executive and writer Mike Steib has described this evolution as the three stages of "learn, earn, and return."[5] In the first stage of our careers, we might focus on building our skills and deepening our knowledge. In the second stage, we might focus more on reaping material success from these early investments. And, in the end, we can dedicate more of our energy to giving back to others—including those just starting out and trying to learn.

Your career doesn't have to follow Steib's pattern—or mine. Your motivations may be entirely different or even moving in the opposite direction. Maybe you started out in the Peace Corps (both "learning" and "returning") and much later in life applied your knowledge to something more lucrative (finally "earning" a bit). Or maybe you needed to earn at an early age, and only had the luxury of going back to school and learning later on.

Everyone's career path is different. There are no bad reasons for working. And yet many of us can't shake the feeling that it would be better not to.

Buddha agreed that finding enlightenment in the working world could be difficult, that it could feel "confining" to many of us, that we could feel "weighed down" by our worldly commitments.[6] But to be clear, he was not contrasting this with resort living. He was comparing both work and family life to going very much the other way—giving up all possessions and attachments. He felt enlightenment was a bit easier as a wandering monk, but he understood that such a path wasn't possible for everyone.

On the other hand, Buddha thought quitting your job to follow your bliss was a *terrible* idea. Sure, chasing what he called "sensual desires" might feel good at first, but in the long run it's more like being "pierced by a dart." In the end, such lives are filled with even more suffering, like water flooding a broken boat.[7]

Many people find this hard to believe. If we enjoy golfing or knitting, yoga or reading, wouldn't we be happier doing those things all the time instead of dragging ourselves into the shop?

Probably not. If you've ever eaten too much ice cream or too many doughnuts (it's possible!), you know you can have too much of a good thing. The problem with lying around all day is that it makes us lazy and restless, and these turn out to be huge obstacles to finding true fulfillment.[8] (We have a whole chapter on this coming up.) Working too little is no better than working too much—and possibly worse. Endlessly chasing pleasure just leads to more distractions, the exact opposite of what we need to truly wake up. Buddha referred to "an honest occupation" as "the highest blessing,"[9] not because he wanted us to work 24/7, but because he saw work as an integral part of a fulfilled life.

But our lives can't be only work. In the same verse, Buddha described learning, practicing a craft, hanging out with good people, and maintaining a family as the highest blessing, too. So, yes, that's a lot of highests! But his point was that there are many important blessings in life, and the real trick is to combine them all.

Our lives are best when they're in balance. This is the real message of Buddha's middle way. Whether we work at home, in an office, or at a factory or a store, work can contribute to that balance. There are as many reasons to work as there are workers. Whatever our reasons, we just need to keep that work in its place.

CHAPTER 2

The Cost of Suffering

IF THERE'S NOTHING WRONG WITH WORKING, AT LEAST in theory, why is work so *hard*?

In Buddha's very first formal sermon, he espoused "Four Noble Truths." We'll talk about all four of these shortly, but for now let's focus on the first one, which is usually translated as: "Life is suffering."

It sounds kind of depressing, but Buddha didn't mean it that way at all. He was merely trying to validate a feeling all of us have at one time or another. Life is difficult. Pain and loss are inevitable. But life is not *only* suffering. There are moments of joy and happiness, too. Most of us are not in constant agony. But all of us face difficulties at some point. And knowing that even the most pleasurable, most rewarding experiences will come to an end leaves them tinged with impending loss.

Some scholars aren't even sure *suffering* is exactly what Buddha meant. Buddha didn't speak English, of course. We're not entirely sure what language he did speak. His teachings come to us in a few ancient Indian languages, including one called Pali, and the word used in that language is *dukkha*. One way to translate *dukkha* is "suffering" or even "pain," and that's why the most common rendering of Buddha's first truth in English is what we just said: "Life is suffering." But others have used the word *stress* instead.[1] So another way to think about Buddha's first truth might be: "Life is really stressful."

For many of us, that's the version that really rings true—especially when we're working.

Study after study confirms that our working lives are full of stress. According to a report by the National Institute for Occupational Safety and Health, 40 percent of US workers find their jobs "very or extremely stressful."[2] The Washington Business Group on Health estimated that "46 percent of all employees are severely stressed to the point of burnout."[3] As far back as 1996, surveys found that 75 percent of American workers were experiencing high levels of job stress at least once a week,[4] and things have probably only gotten worse since.

It's not just Americans, either. A recent European study found that 27.5 percent of workers there suffered from increased fatigue, resulting from workplace stress.[5] A survey of women working in Sweden found that 38 percent perceived their jobs as stressful.[6] Sweden! If even the Swedes can't chill out, we must be in real trouble.

All this stress has very real costs. Early estimates of the total societal costs of workplace stress back in the 1990s were as much as 10 percent of GNP.[7] Today, in the United States, that would represent over $1 trillion dollars! The direct cost in lost revenue alone from workplace stress is estimated at $150 billion.[8] Worldwide, the International Labor

Organization estimates the cost of workplace stress at 1–3.5 percent of total world GDP.[9]

And it's not just financial cost. In his book *Dying for a Paycheck*, Stanford professor Jeffrey Pfeffer explains that workplace stress probably leads to more health issues and more avoidable deaths than secondhand smoke. Stress in most offices is so severe that "White-collar jobs are often as stressful and unhealthful as manual labor, [and] frequently more so."[10] The American Institute of Stress estimates that "75 percent to 90 percent of all doctor visits are now stress-related."[11]

But it doesn't have to be this way. Work doesn't have to make us miserable. And when we find ways to be happy at work, everyone benefits.

We've known for at least two decades that happiness increases our productivity at work.[12] One study found the volunteers whose mood was boosted by watching a funny video performed significantly better on a math task designed to simulate workplace thinking.[13] Those same researchers found that a "bad life event" (like a death in the family or a serious illness) reduced people's performance by about 10 percent—even if it occurred two years before. It's just hard to do good work when you're sad, and much easier when you're in a cheerful mood.

A survey of many recent studies concluded that happiness improves creativity, and that "Positive attitudes and experiences are associated with beneficial consequences for both employees and organizations."[14] A large-scale longitudinal study in Canada found similar results.[15] As the Canadians researcher put it quite simply: "Happy people were more productive" and "People were more productive when they were happier."

We often think that career success will lead us to happiness, and many of us tolerate bad days, bad bosses, and truly bad jobs with that hope in mind. But we may have this backward. What if being unhappy on the job just makes us less productive and ultimately less successful?

In an exhaustive review of the scientific literature, three California researchers concluded exactly that: "Happy people receive higher earnings, exhibit better performance, and obtain more favorable supervisor evaluations than their less happy peers."[16] They came to this conclusion after reviewing decades of "cross-sectional, longitudinal, and experimental research"— essentially every possible way of studying the question.

Their bottom line was very clear: "Happiness precedes and leads to career success." Not the other way around.

To summarize, many of us suffer on the job, and this suffering exacts real costs—on our health and on our employers. At the same time, happy workers are not only, well, happier, but also more productive and more valuable to their employers. Happiness is its own reward, but it can lead us to more success on the job, too.

So how do we become happy? Is there some magic key that can unlock our happiness and all those benefits? That's what Buddha set out to find.

CHAPTER 3

Buddhism Was a Start-up

WE'VE TALKED A BIT ABOUT BUDDHA'S LIFE, BUT WE GLOS-sed over some pretty important questions: Why did Buddha start Buddhism? And why did this particular spiritual start-up end up lasting so long?

There turns out to be a bit of controversy about exactly when Buddha lived. No one tried to pin down the date until centuries later, and the stories of his life don't mention any current events that we can cross-check. Buddhist scholars from various countries have come up with different dates, based on the information we do have, and these vary by over 100 years.[1] To be honest, I find their arguments a bit hard to follow—a lot apparently hinges on precisely how many years elapsed between Buddha's death and the rule of a certain Indian king, because that king met some ancient Greeks who were better at calendars. But if you say he lived around 500 BCE, no one will call you a liar, and you probably won't be too far off.

That's a long time ago. A lot has changed in the last two-and-a-half millennia, making the Buddhist community—called the sangha—the world's oldest surviving institution.[2] No company, no university, no government, and no standing army has survived as long. Buddha's sangha has outlasted them all.

Of course, before there was a sangha practicing Buddhism, there was just Buddha. Regardless of precisely when, everyone agrees that Buddha was born a prince in what is now Nepal, and raised nearby, probably in northeast India. He led a highly sheltered life in a beautiful palace, surrounded by every imaginable luxury of the era. (Think sumptuous food and fancy clothes, but, alas, no Nintendo or Legos.) His mother died in childbirth, but her sister stepped in and raised him as her own, as the king's second wife. He had a happy childhood, married young, and had a child, all while secluded in these lavish grounds dotted with beautiful lotus ponds. He had three mansions, one for each of the Indian seasons. He spent the four-month rainy season, when it was too wet to go outside, holed up with only female servants and companions.[3] (Make of this what you will—we're told they were "musicians.")

But then, around the time of his 29th birthday, he ran away to become a wandering ascetic. The story is that he convinced a faithful servant to sneak his chariot out into the surrounding village, and there he witnessed for the first time the ravages of sickness, old age, and death.[4] He realized that life is not all fun and games and pleasure palaces, and decided to pursue a purely spiritual life. He spent six years crisscrossing the Indian countryside, practicing all sorts of austerities under various notable teachers. He tried everything from fasting to self-flagellation, anything that was the opposite of his old life of luxury, before he got fed up with that life, too, convinced that it wasn't bringing him answers to life's big questions, either.

At last he decided to just sit by himself and meditate all night, and that's when he had his big epiphany, his awakening. That's when he earned the title of Buddha, which literally means the Awakened One.

We'll talk more about what he discovered that night in the next chapter. But the point here is that Buddha's first inclination was to stop right there. He had done it. He had accomplished his great goal after all those years of effort. He was enlightened now. He could finally cease his endless searching.

He thought about teaching but decided, no, he was good with just being a Buddha and not a teacher.

In a sense, his reason for *not* teaching was the same reason many of us have for not trying something new: He thought he would fail.

The way Buddha himself explained it later, he felt his newfound path was "hard to see and hard to understand," and that "if I were to teach…, others would not understand me, and that would be wearying and troublesome to me."[5] In other words, teaching the dharma—his newfound truth—would be hard, it probably wouldn't work, and that would be a huge bummer, even for an enlightened Buddha. "Considering thus," he concluded, "my mind inclined to inaction rather than to teaching."

I think we can all understand where he was coming from. None of us like to fail. And trying something new is always a risk.

Legend has it that it took divine intervention to change his mind. The god Brahma descended to earth and begged Buddha to share his wisdom. Perhaps not everyone would understand, Brahma agreed, but some would. And those precious successes would make up for any failures. After some pleading, Buddha was convinced.

Once Buddha started teaching, he could hardly stop. In the end he taught for 45 years, continuing right up until his death. (His last lecture was delivered from his deathbed.) But, like a lot of us, it just took a little pushing to get him over his self-doubts.

So why have Buddha's teachings survived so long, when even Buddha himself wasn't sure anyone would understand them?

I think there are a few reasons. First of all, Buddha was practical. He spoke about the world as it exists around us, the world as we know it ourselves. He tried to help people solve real-world problems that anyone could understand. He gave very practical exercises—many of which we'll try here—for how to live a happier and more awakened life.

When asked more abstract questions, Buddha often brushed them aside. For example, he refused to say whether or not he believed in an afterlife.[6] It's just not important, he argued. He compared it to a man struck by an arrow, who won't let a surgeon treat him until he knows the name and clan of the one who shot it, or whether he was tall or short, or where he was from, or what form of bow he used, and so on. These may be interesting questions, perhaps, but the most important thing is to take out the arrow. For all of us suffering in this world, whether or not there's a next world is just idle curiosity.

Second, Buddha was flexible. He tried all sorts of different approaches before he settled on what became his path. And he studied with contemporary masters around him and learned what he could from them before setting off on his own.

He rejected the rigidity of India's caste system, insisting that good and bad qualities "are scattered indiscriminately among the four castes"[7] and that anyone could become enlightened. He welcomed "outcasts" and "untouchables" into his community of followers, insisting that "one is not an outcast by birth," but only through immoral deeds.[8] His path was open to anyone, anywhere.

And although Buddha made lots of rules (that was part of being practical), in his final sermon he suggested that future students could abolish any of the "minor" ones, and left it up to them to decide which were minor.[9] He seemed willing to adapt his teachings to different times and places, and to admit when he was wrong. (He first refused to ordain women, but eventually his foster mother convinced him.) He was open to new experiences, and kept meditating all his life, practicing what he preached.

Third, Buddha was positive. Like any good entrepreneur, Buddha believed in himself. He believed that he could find a path beyond suffering. And after that first hesitancy to teach, we don't see a lot of prevarication or indecision on his part. Buddha also believed in us. "Dwell with yourselves as your own island, with yourselves as your own refuge," he told his followers, shortly before his death.[10] Trust yourself. That's a message many of us want—and need—to hear.

But being practical, flexible, and positive was no guarantee of success. Lots of people have those qualities—and lots probably did 2,500 years ago, too. Most of those people never start something nearly as successful as Buddhism.

Like any start-up, the ultimate success of Buddhism depended on the quality of the product. A great founder can only take you so far. More than anything else, the success of Buddhism the start-up depended on the product Buddha discovered. Buddha saw a problem—suffering—and he found a solution. And that solution worked.

From that point on, it was almost easy. A product that miraculous just about sells itself.

CHAPTER 4

Buddha's Big Idea

AFTER HIS GREAT AWAKENING, BUDDHA TAUGHT FOR 45 years. His lectures covered everything from exercise and sleep to eating and mental concentration. He probably had at least something to say on almost every topic you can imagine. But none of that would have mattered if he hadn't figured out one thing that went to the heart of every human life: *Awakening is possible.*

To Buddha's mind, most of us drift through life half-asleep. We're going through the motions, enjoying ourselves sometimes, but we're not all there. We're not really paying attention. And this is a tragedy! We're letting this life slip away half-lived.

Nowhere is this more apparent for most of us than at work. We daydream at our desks. We count the minutes (or hours!) in meetings. We make endless plans for what we'll do next, instead of focusing on what we're doing now.

Buddha's big idea was that it doesn't have to be this way. It's possible for us to wake up and live a full life right now—even on the job.

The very name *Buddha* means "Awakened One," so the whole basis of what we now call Buddhism is that at least *someone* once realized awakening. What Buddhists call the "three treasures" of Buddhism are the Buddha, the original Awakened One; the dharma, his teachings; and the sangha, or his community of followers. Without that first experience of awakening, there's really nothing.

Before I explain more about what Buddha meant, I should say more about how we know *anything* about what this former Indian prince did or said 2,500 years ago. When I quote from Buddha's words here, I'm quoting from the written accounts of his teachings. The Buddha's lectures weren't recorded, of course, and he never wrote anything down himself. It's not entirely clear that he was even literate.[1] Writing in those days was considered a specialized profession, and not a necessary part of a general education, even for royalty like him. There are no accounts in the Buddhist scriptures of him ever reading or writing.

Months after Buddha's death, it's said that 500 fully enlightened followers assembled at the invitation of a local king to discuss the teachings and ensure consensus throughout the sangha. They took turns reciting Buddha's lectures and committing them to memory. They were then passed down orally for several generations as Buddhism began to spread. Humans are surprisingly good at this sort of memorization. (I can still recite the Preamble to the United States Constitution, which I learned in grade school and have only repeated maybe a dozen times in 30 years.) These monks and nuns had special training and probably recited the texts often to keep them fresh. There were two more of these "Buddhist Councils," held approximately 100 and then 200 years after Buddha's passing, again to ensure agreement on the teachings and to resolve any discrepancies.[2] But still—we can be pretty sure that errors crept in.

By the time anything was written down, the teachings had spread too far for all the followers to meet. A Fourth Buddhist Council was held in Sri Lanka, sometime around 100 CE, and here the Buddha's words were transcribed into Pali, an ancient Indian language, and written on palm leaves. But the Buddha didn't speak Pali, although whatever he spoke was probably closely related to that language. So even this version of the Buddhist canon was a translation. And we don't have any of those documents because palm leaves, as you might suspect, are pretty fragile, so we have copies of copies of copies, and so on. The oldest copies we have are from at least a thousand years later.[3]

Others elsewhere in Asia also started writing things down around the same time, often in other ancient Indian languages. These versions were eventually taken to China and Tibet, where they were then translated into *those* languages. Based on fragments of manuscripts and even stone carvings found around India, we know that many of the earliest translations have been lost.* In other cases, we end up with two or

---

* At least so far. The oldest surviving Buddhist scriptures we now have were discovered in Pakistan only 25 years ago, written on birch bark and buried in clay jars.[4] Who knows what we may find next? So please don't throw away old jars.

three versions of the same lecture in different languages, and can compare these to try to discern what the original might have been.[5]

This is a long-winded way of saying that anything I'm quoting here in English is at best a distant copy of a translation of a translation of a long-ago memorization, first written down many centuries after the Buddha lived. That's all we have.

But according to these writings, Buddha didn't set out to become "awakened" at all. Back when he was just a confused prince, what he really wanted was to understand suffering. Specifically, from the time he had his first exposure to sickness, old age, and death during that secret excursion outside the palace, Buddha kept asking himself how we go on living knowing that pain and loss are unavoidable. How can we stay sane in a world filled with suffering?

Remember, his parents had an easy answer for him, one we've probably all tried ourselves at one time or another: denial. For them, the simple way to overcome suffering was to avoid it at all cost. That's why they coddled and sheltered him so much. They thought if they could fill their son's life with comfort and pleasure, he would never have to suffer at all.

It didn't work, of course, just as it probably hasn't worked for you. Avoiding our problems doesn't make them go away. There's nothing wrong with treating ourselves to something special now and then, but the effects of even the best retail therapy or spa treatment are usually very short-lived.

Buddha figured out why denial and avoidance don't really work. The problem with chasing after fun is that it never lasts. And as soon as we realize that it won't last, it stops being quite so much fun anymore.

On the other hand, if you surround yourself with suffering, that doesn't work, either. Buddha tried that, too, for six years after he left home. He tried practices so extreme that he almost died. But all he accomplished by beating himself up was becoming even more miserable. Wallowing in suffering doesn't diminish it, either.

This was the great truth Buddha awakened to, the big idea that made him the Buddha: that the only way to overcome suffering is to find the middle way between those extremes. Instead of running away from pain or running toward it, you sort of accept it. And by accepting that life involves a certain amount of pain and unpleasantness, you rob the pain of its power. That is, it's all about balance.

How exactly does balance beat suffering? In his first lecture, after announcing his middle way, Buddha proceeded to describe his Four Noble Truths. Again, we don't know *exactly* how he described these at the time, but the translations we have are roughly the following:

Life is suffering.
The cause of suffering is desire.

The way to end suffering is to end desire.
The way to end desire is through the Noble Eightfold Path.

I've mentioned that last part—the eightfold path—and we'll talk more about it in the next chapter. For now, let's focus on the first three.

One way to think about those first three truths is that we suffer because we want things to be different. The cause of suffering isn't actually pain or bad luck—it's dissatisfaction. It's wanting stuff, craving stuff. We don't suffer because bad things happen; we suffer because we don't get what we want.

That's not to say that pain is good or pleasant. It isn't. But this unpleasantness is not the cause of suffering. Resisting it is the cause of suffering. And while Buddha learned that pain can never be completely avoided, suffering can still be overcome.

You sometimes see this message summarized with the phrase *Suffering is optional*.[6] I think that's a pretty good way to think about it. When something painful happens to us, we don't just feel the immediate pain—we also have feelings about the pain. We're angry about our pain, maybe frustrated or resentful, even vengeful sometimes. So then we have two unpleasant feelings—a physical one and a mental one. Buddha described this as like being struck by two arrows.* The first arrow we can't avoid—pain hurts, whether

---

* Yes, another arrow metaphor. (See the previous chapter for the first one.) It seems safe to assume that getting shot by an arrow was a lot more common in Buddha's time.

we want it to or not. But the second arrow is our own choice. We can duck. Even if we suffer from the pain, we don't need to suffer *about* the pain. By living a life of balance, neither fighting nor courting pain, we avoid these second arrows.

All of this applies to us at work, too. No matter how hard we try, obstacles will always come up at work. We may miss out on a new job or a promotion. We may have to deal with a difficult colleague or boss or customer. We may be up against an impossible deadline or have a terrible shift. We don't need to be out there looking for these difficulties, but we can't entirely avoid them, either.

Buddha's advice is not that we should be happy when we run into these problems, but just that we should accept that they happen and move on. The key to awakening is not to avoid problems or to ignore them. Living in denial or living in a dream is not the answer.

If all that sounds easier said than done, it is. But Buddha also found an important technique to help us along the way. That's what we'll discuss next.

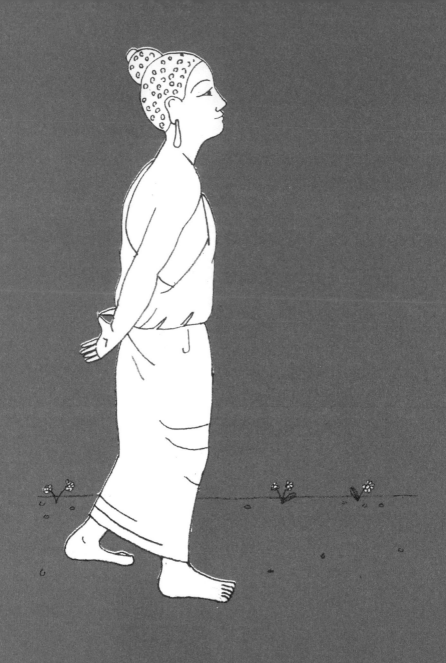

PART 2

PRACTICES

CHAPTER 5

Paying Attention

THE SINGLE MOST IMPORTANT THING YOU CAN DO AT work is the same as the single most important thing Buddha said you should do in life: Pay attention. In other words, practice mindfulness.

You probably hear a lot of talk about mindfulness these days. Mindfulness is taught in schools and companies. The National Library of Medicine lists over 3,000 scientific publications with "mindfulness" in the title. Although the first of these papers dates back to 1982 (and it's a good one!),[1] 2,963 of them were published in just the last 10 years.

For many people, mindfulness, meditation, and Buddhism are all synonymous. I can understand why: Buddha had his great awakening after an all-night meditation, and you probably have the sense that mindfulness and meditation are somehow connected. But they aren't the same. And understanding the difference is essential to understanding why mindfulness is so important to work and life in the first place.

Mindfulness was part of Buddha's teachings from the beginning. It's mentioned in his very first sermon, usually called the Deer Park Sermon because, well, it was given in a deer park, at a forest clearing frequented by deer. But mindfulness doesn't come up right away. Buddha starts by describing the "middle way," which is what he calls the path of avoiding the two extremes he had followed up until that point. As we've discussed, Buddha's life was something of a pendulum for his first 35 years. But the key to awakening is not to try to hide from suffering, as he did as a prince for his first 29 years, or to wallow in suffering, as he did as an ascetic for the next 6 years, but instead to navigate in between. You can think of this as not avoiding suffering and not courting suffering, but accepting it and dealing with it and moving on from it.

As this first sermon continues, Buddha gets into a little more detail and explains the eight parts to this middle-way path. We need to cultivate right views, right intention, right speech, right action, right livelihood, right effort, right mindfulness, and right concentration. Buddha doesn't go into much detail beyond enumerating these eight things, and here at the outset it isn't clear that he considers mindfulness any more important than the other parts of the path.

Then he walks us through what we now call the Four Noble Truths, that while suffering exists and is inevitable, it is caused by our endless striving, and there is a path to accept and ultimately overcome it. This path is that same eightfold path we just listed.

That's it. That's the end of the first talk—after which, the ascetics who heard it, every one of them, experienced awakening, by the way. Mindfulness is mentioned twice, but only toward the end of his eight important parts of practice. And meditation is not mentioned explicitly at all. If all you knew about Buddhism was that first sermon, you'd know it was about overcoming suffering, but you probably wouldn't think mindfulness and meditation were all that important.

But as Buddha later expounded on these initial ideas, mindfulness started to take on a more central position. He gave several whole sermons on mindfulness alone. He came to declare the foundations of mindfulness to be "the direct path…for the attainment of the true way" and the realization of nirvana.[2]

Why would right mindfulness be any more important than right speech or right action? If you step outside the Buddhist context for a minute, this isn't obvious at all. Isn't mindfulness a state of mind? Surely our actions cause more suffering than our thinking. We've all had the experience of causing suffering, either to ourselves or others, either intentionally or unintentionally, with our words and actions. But can we really cause suffering with our minds?

The answer is yes, we can. And we do. All the time.

Let's start with what mindfulness itself even means. One modern Buddhist scholar describes it as "the clear and single-minded awareness of what actually happens to us in and at the successive moments of perception."[3] A more psychological definition would be "the state of being attentive to and aware of what is taking place in the present."[4] In the absolute simplest terms, as we said at the start of this chapter, mindfulness means paying attention.

That attention is the linchpin for the rest of the eightfold path. There's no way to cultivate right speech without paying attention to how we are speaking. There's no way to cultivate right action without paying attention to what we're doing. Without mindfulness, we're stuck. It's like trying to follow Buddha's path in our sleep.

That's the connection between mindfulness and Buddhism. Buddhism is our modern word for Buddha's teaching, what's traditionally called the dharma. Put another way, Buddhism is the articulation of Buddha's path to awakening. And mindfulness is what makes it possible to follow that path.

Maybe the primacy of mindfulness wasn't obvious to Buddha when he first started teaching. Or maybe it was so obvious that he didn't feel the need to explain it. But this is why we focus so much on mindfulness today in Buddhist practice—because mindfulness is the key that unlocks his whole path.

Mindfulness is essential at work, too. Your job may seem mindless at times, but I assure you that if it really was, you wouldn't be doing it. These days, just about anything that can be automated *is* automated. If you're doing a job, it's because someone felt we needed someone doing it who was paying attention.

This is backed by research. Studies have shown that developing mindfulness improves job performance across a wide range of industries and professions, including restaurant servers, supervisors and middle managers, nurses, psychotherapists, and even nuclear power plant operators.[5] One test that offered a one-hour-per-week mindfulness class for eight weeks to nurses in a high-stress Intensive-Care Unit found "engagement and resiliency increase[d] significantly" among the participants.[6] In environments like this, where employee performance has stark real-world consequences, the authors noted that mindfulness "not only improves the lives of individuals, but potentially the lives that they touch through their work." Even a study in the US Army found that mindfulness training "may protect against functional impairments associated with high-stress contexts."[7] (If you're wondering whether Buddha would approve of teaching mindfulness to soldiers, the study's authors also posit that mindfulness "could provide greater cognitive resources for soldiers to act ethically and effectively in the morally ambiguous and emotionally challenging counterinsurgency environment.")

But mindfulness isn't just for trauma nurses and soldiers. Even in more typical workplaces, mindfulness has been shown to improve "creativity, innovation, resilience, work engagement, productivity, communication skills, reduced conflict, absenteeism, and turnover."[8] A study of 238 employees at the health insurer Aetna found that mindfulness training improved productivity there and reduced employee-perceived stress.[9] Companies as diverse as Target, General Mills, and Intel have offered mindfulness programs to their employees and seen positive results.[10]

So if mindfulness is so great, where do we get it? That's the subject of our next chapter. It turns out you don't have to work for a company like Google that teaches mindfulness right there at the office. The most important thing you can do for work may be something you can do at home.

CHAPTER 6

Meditate Like a Buddha

MINDFULNESS IS HARD. THE WORLD IS FILLED WITH DIS-tractions. How many times have you picked up your phone since you picked up this book? How many texts will you send or receive before you finish this chapter?

But it's not just cell phones and screens that distract us. Mindfulness was hard 2,500 years ago. Even then, Buddha worried that people were so consumed with their own distractions (he called them "attachments") that they would never understand his teachings. "It is hard for such a generation to see this truth," he lamented—words likely echoed by every teacher in every generation since.[1] And keep in mind that Buddha's troublesome generation didn't just live before cell phones and computers and television and radio. They lived before *paper*—and still mindlessness and distraction felt like insurmountable problems.

So how do we develop mindfulness? We know now how important it is, but where do we get it? How do we learn to cut through all those distractions?

Buddha had a very simple answer for this: meditation. Meditation is the way we practice mindfulness.

I mean *practice* here literally. It's the same way we might use finger exercises to practice piano. If you ever tried learning piano as a kid—or if you've had the misfortune of listening to a kid practice more recently—you know that practicing piano is *not* the same as playing piano. When we practice, we might hit the same few notes over and over again. We're developing muscle memory in our hands and training our minds to read the notes. But that's very different from playing music.

It's the same with driving. You might practice in an empty parking lot or try to parallel park between two cones on a quiet street. But you're not really *driving* until you go out into traffic.

So, just to be clear, real awakening doesn't happen on a meditation cushion. Awakening happens out here in the world. Awakening is about how we live our lives after we get up from the cushion. We meditate to prepare ourselves for that.

Buddha gave very detailed instructions on how to meditate. He devoted whole lectures to various techniques and modern teachers have written whole books on individual lectures.[2] The different schools of Buddhism have developed slightly different styles over the centuries, but most start with a few basic guidelines: Find a quiet place, sit in an upright posture, and focus on your breathing.

Buddha suggests a few quiet places you could try: in the forest, at the root of a tree, or in an empty hut.[3] These days any quiet room will do. In the Zen tradition, meditators typically sit facing a wall. The goal is to minimize distractions. Again, it's a bit like practicing driving in that empty parking lot. You start by making things as easy on yourself as possible.

The traditional posture is the lotus position, legs crossed so that each foot rests on the opposite thigh. If you can manage that, great. (You've probably been doing yoga—also, great.) If not, you can try the half lotus, where one foot rests on your thigh and the other gets tucked in below it. If that's too much of a stretch, there's the so-called Burmese posture, with both feet crossed in front of you on the floor. All of these are easier if you sit on a small pillow or cushion.

You can also kneel or even sit on a chair. The goal is to sit upright, spine fairly straight, so that your body feels fully supported. A common technique is to imagine the crown of your head being pulled toward the ceiling, your spine gently stretched, and then released, so that each vertebra rests comfortably on the one below it. If you're doing it right, it should take very little effort to keep your body upright.

Now you're ready to start meditating. Start by setting a timer. *This is important.* It's very hard to meditate if you have to keep checking the time to know when you're done. You can use the timer on your phone or an old-school kitchen timer if you have one, or you can download a specialized app.* Whatever you choose, I suggest starting with five minutes.

Take three deep breaths. With each breath in, be aware that

---

* There are many! I particularly like the *Insight Timer* app, which is both free and fantastic: https://insighttimer.com/.

you're breathing in. With each breath out, be aware that you're breathing out. After these first three, just breathe normally. But keep your awareness on your breath. Be aware of long breaths and short breaths. Try to notice each and every one.

One way Buddha suggested you do this is by narrating each breath to yourself.[4] Breathing in, you say (to yourself, silently), "I am breathing in." Breathing out, you say to yourself, "I am breathing out." Taking a long breath, you say, "I am taking a long breath." Taking a short breath, you say, "I am taking a short breath." This helps keep your mind from wandering and focuses your awareness.

This is not just a mental awareness. It's a physical awareness, too. You should *feel* yourself breathing. You should notice the way the breath enters your body and leaves your body. You should feel it against your mouth or nose. You should notice the way your chest rises and falls. You should *feel* your chest rise and fall.

It's common these days to hear people talk about how certain seemingly physical activities— like running or tennis or golf—are, to a large extent, mental. But the opposite is also true. We tend to think of meditation as a purely mental exercise, a way of quieting the mind, but it is also a physical activity. Meditation is not just some way of thinking; it is something we *do*, with our bodies as much as our minds.

Why start with the breath? You can think of your breathing as a sort of biological metronome, establishing a basic drumbeat of your existence. You might think your heart rate could serve this function, but most of us aren't aware of our individual heartbeats. Our breathing seems to lie at the sweet spot of being both ever-present and yet fully knowable, discernable, in a way that our other bodily functions are not.

If this all sounds very easy, then you probably haven't sat down to try it yet. Most people find it difficult at first. The mind wanders. We start thinking about an annoying thing that happened at work or an errand we need to run later or an old flame from college or a new flame online. We're sure we just heard our phone buzz and wonder who might be texting us. At some point we realize that we haven't noticed our breathing in who knows how long. We desperately want to look at the timer and see how much longer we're supposed to sit here.

That's OK. When you notice that your mind has wandered, just go back to your breath. It doesn't matter if this happens one time or a hundred times. Don't beat yourself up. Just take another breath.

Once we've gotten comfortable watching our breath in this way, Buddha encourages us to cultivate mindfulness of the entire body. When we sit, we should be aware of our whole body sitting. We should feel each point where our body touches the ground beneath us. We should feel our legs folded against each other. We should feel our hands resting on our lap. We should notice the air against our skin, and *feel* this air, warm or cold, still or moving. Our awareness should include every part of us.

How powerful are these mindfulness meditations? Buddha thought they were pretty powerful! In one sutra, he starts by stating that anyone who practices these mindfulness meditation exercises for just seven years will be guaranteed nirvana.[5] That's pretty good! I mean, think about it. Seven years might sound long, but we spend twelve years in grade school, four just in high school, and what do we have to show for that? (Try starting a conversation using your high school Spanish and you'll see what I mean.) Many of us spend four or five or more years in college just to prepare for a job, and still come out feeling unprepared. Buddha is saying that in *just seven years* of practice, we can do so much more than that. We can unlock the key to overcome all suffering. We can literally find nirvana.

And then here, despite his enlightened state, Buddha establishes himself as a truly terrible negotiator. Because immediately—right in the middle of that lecture!—he starts bargaining against himself. Maybe, actually, six years would be enough. Or maybe five, he suggests. Or four. And he gets all the way down to one year. A single year! And then he decides even that is too much, and admits maybe just seven months would be enough. Or six? And he negotiates himself all the way down to one month, and then half a month, until finally, he settles on seven days. And that's it. That's his final offer.

That's as low as he'll go. If we can fully practice mindfulness meditation for just seven days, we are guaranteed awakening.

That's a pretty awesome deal. But how is it possible? How can practicing meditation for seven days or even seven years bring us closer to that awakening?

Again, it's like the analogy with the piano. All those finger exercises may sound monotonous, but they work their magic when you move on to real music. Similarly, over time, by practicing mindfulness this way in meditation, we start to bring that mindfulness into our daily lives. We may not be aware of every breath or every motion throughout the day, but we stop sleepwalking through our days, too.

Gradually we start to take our mindfulness practice off the cushion. Buddha says when we walk, we should be aware that we're walking. When we stand, we should be aware that we're standing. When we sit again or lie down, we should be aware of our bodies there, too—our whole bodies. Walking, we should feel the way each part of our foot touches the earth, the way our weight shifts with every movement, the way our body responds to every step and every breath. The goal, Buddha said, is to become one "who acts with full awareness when walking, standing, sitting, falling asleep, waking up, talking, and keeping silent."[6] That awareness we cultivate in meditation starts to manifest itself out there, in the real world. In other words, this mindfulness begins to permeate our lives—at home, at work, and everywhere.

That mindfulness makes the rest of Buddha's eightfold path possible out there, too. We start practicing right speech because we're mindful of the way our speech affects others. We start practicing right action because we're mindful of the consequences of our actions. And on and on. Mindfulness is the key to the rest of the path. Everything good flows from there. As Buddha taught: "Speak or act with a peaceful mind, and happiness follows, like a never-departing shadow."[7]

To experience this for yourself, commit right now to a daily meditation practice. The most important thing is to get into a routine of meditating every day. After you're comfortable with the 5-minute sessions we've described, I recommend that you increase to 10 minutes a day. Even on your busiest days, you can probably wake up 10 minutes earlier or go to bed 10 minutes later. (The average American spends over 8 minutes daily in the shower,[8] so, worst case, you could borrow a few minutes there.)

If you can work your way up to 20 minutes, that's wonderful. That's what I do most days. I think 20 minutes is plenty of time to develop a strong meditation practice. If 20 minutes is more than you can manage, then stick with 10. Maybe you can add a 20-minute session on the weekends or on another day off.

Is 10 minutes a day really enough? Some would say there's no such thing as enough! The Dalai Lama still meditates several hours each day, and he's been doing it his whole life.[9]

Lots of other less famous long-term practitioners also meditate for long periods. But most of us would find that pretty challenging, and most people notice real benefits from *much* shorter periods. Like physical exercise, every little bit helps. (More on that soon!) It's much better to carve out *some* time to meditate every day than to promise yourself grand plans for long meditations that never actually happen.

To be clear, I can't promise you any magic after just seven days. To be honest, I never fully understood why Buddha said that. Because it isn't easy to bring mindfulness into our daily lives. It's hard, and it takes both practice and patience. But the key is that it's possible. That's the real lesson of Buddha's life story. It's the record of one person who managed to walk this path. He was able to develop enough mindfulness to truly wake up. He realized enlightenment. And if he can do it, we can, too.

CHAPTER 7

The Problem with Expertise

IF YOU'RE NEW TO MEDITATION, THE EXERCISES IN THE LAST chapter probably felt a bit unnatural and uncomfortable. Most of us feel awkward doing something—anything—for the first time. We worry that we're doing it wrong. We're embarrassed by our ignorance. Maybe, in this case, sitting all alone in a room, your legs folded in this unusual way, your hands in your lap, you felt a little ridiculous.

Buddha would tell you that's just fine.

We spend much of our lives striving to be experts—especially at work. We like to feel competent and capable. We want respect from our colleagues and praise from our supervisors. We don't like making mistakes. But it turns out there is real danger in all that apparent expertise.

Back in medieval Japan, the great Zen master Eihei Dogen had a different view of being a beginner. He worried that what we think of as experience and expertise often leads to carelessness and inattention. He saw a certain power in that uncomfortable feeling we have when we're first starting out and have no idea what we're doing. He called that anxious, empty mind-set "beginner's mind." He went so far as to say that sitting in meditation with beginner's mind is sitting like a true Buddha—and he saw great risk in losing that beginner's mind as we continued our meditation training.[1]

This idea is not unique to Buddhism. Most of the world's religions seem to have some similar concept, some notion of a "basic wisdom" inherent in all of us.[2] But it seems to have found its most complete and explicit expression in the school of Zen Buddhism that master Dogen brought to Japan. Hundreds of years later, the modern Zen master Shunryu Suzuki expanded on and popularized Dogen's idea in a famous series of talks he gave to his American students in California. "The goal of practice," he told them, "is always to keep your beginner's mind."[3] Basically, he taught that we should never become an expert! He explained this odd advice like this:

> This does not mean a closed mind, but actually an empty mind and a ready mind. If your mind is empty, it is always ready for anything; it is open to everything. In the beginner's mind there are many possibilities; in the expert's mind there are few.[4]

The most obvious time beginner's mind comes into play at work is when we're starting a new assignment or embarking on a new job. Suddenly we're not feeling so competent any more. We're not sure exactly what we're supposed to do. We're almost guaranteed to get something wrong. We're tiptoeing around, certain that everyone can sense our ignorance. We feel like the new kid in middle school who doesn't know where to eat lunch.

Yet we can use this nervous energy, this alertness, to our advantage. Just because we're uncomfortable in a novel situation, we don't have to be uncomfortable *about* being uncomfortable. Everyone you work with had a first day, too. None of us are born experts in anything, and some of the people around you probably know less than they think they do. The true opposite of wisdom, after all, is not ignorance but arrogance. Ignorance is a perfectly respectable state of being. Ignorance is the origin of all eventual knowledge. Arrogance is where the danger lies. The wonderful thing about being a beginner is that you know what you don't know. The expert has often forgotten.

Yet it's even more important to cultivate beginner's mind when you're *not* just starting out in something new. When you've worked at a job for a long time, it can easily become rote and mechanical. We feel like we're just punching the clock, going through the motions. We can become one of those arrogant experts peering skeptically at the newcomers. That's where carelessness seeps in, whether born of boredom or conceit. That's when we have to make an extra effort to regain our beginner's mind.

One way to try to snap out of monotony is simply to take a break—and we have a whole chapter on that coming up next. Another is to change tasks. Many of us have different sorts of work we need to do throughout the day, the week, or even the year. One way to cultivate beginner's mind is to rotate through these different tasks more frequently and give yourself the literal experience of doing something new more often.

On the other hand, sometimes reclaiming your beginner's mind is as easy as getting a change of scene. When I'm stuck on a problem or feeling unmotivated, I sometimes take my laptop to a new part of the building and work there. (This has the added benefit of making me harder to find, so I'm less likely to be disturbed.) Some companies have taken this to the extreme, eliminating assigned workspaces altogether. As with everything, the key is balance. It's often helpful to be in your familiar space, with everything just the way you like it. (My desk always looks like a mess, but I know exactly where everything is and can find it quickly.) But when your work starts feeling stale, you can move somewhere unfamiliar to shake things up.

Beginner's mind is not the same as imposter's syndrome, typically defined as the "experience of feeling incompetent and of having deceived others about one's abilities."[5] That's a terrible feeling. First observed among female college students, it was initially assumed to affect mostly women. Something about feeling as if you *look* out of place seems to bring with it the fear that maybe you really *are* out of place—and will soon be exposed as an imposter. But these days we understand that this is also quite common among men. Many of us feel at any moment that our colleagues will realize that we're frauds, that we don't really know what we're doing at all.

The most important thing to remember when you start having these feelings is that they are extremely common. Almost everyone I know at work suffers from imposter's syndrome at times—myself certainly included. You are not alone. Many if not most of your colleagues are having the same doubts you are. Yet you are where you are through the results of all your past actions—what Buddha would call karma. Luck may have played some role, but it played a role for everyone else, too. You deserve to be where you are as much as anyone.*

Beginner's mind can also help you combat imposter's syndrome. Instead of desperately trying to hide our supposed incompetence, we actively cultivate an openness to learning and discovery. Instead of fearing to admit there's anything we don't know, we are eager to find the limits of our knowledge. That's the best way to learn, and to help those around us learn, too. When we acknowledge our limits up front, we don't have to live in fear of later being unmasked.

We can apply the beginner's mind approach to any field. The University of Pennsylvania biomedical researcher Albert J. Stunkard studied with Shunryu Suzuki early in life, and tried to bring a beginner's mind to his long, pioneering career investigating eating disorders. He described the application

---

* In fact, the only people who don't seem to have these fears are those so self-absorbed that they can't imagine themselves as anything but successful—exactly the ones who could use a dose of self-doubt.

of beginner's mind to his research as "taking each moment as it arises as a moment of discovery and giving [himself] wholly to that moment."[6] Across the country in California, software architect Arlo Belshee applied these same principles to coding. In dividing up the work on a major software project, he found that "the optimal worker for a task is the one who is the least skillful in that task," because "he tries more approaches, and tries them rapidly," and so "is more likely to succeed at a task than one who thinks he understands."[7] In other words, the least skillful coder brings the most beginner's mind to the work.

Belshee's observation points to yet another approach we can bring to reclaim our beginner's mind: working with new people. If you're an expert in what you do, try teaming up with someone just starting out. You will learn a lot by explaining the work to them, and seeing it through their eyes for the first time. Perhaps you've had the experience of showing out-of-town guests around your neighborhood, and suddenly seeing it in a whole new way. I love giving tours around my office for similar reasons—I start to notice all the little things I like about the building that I otherwise start to take for granted. When I'm assembling a new technical team, I like to seed it with recent college graduates because I know they'll ask great questions and force us to think hard about the right approach, rather than just repeating whatever worked last time.

If you're the novice, you can do the opposite and start

collaborating with an old-timer. You'll learn from them, but they'll learn from you, too.

A final approach to stay fresh at work is to force yourself to become a beginner outside of the workplace. You can take up a new hobby or learn a challenging new skill. For example, the highly successful English professor Sheryl Fontaine described regaining her beginner's mind by studying martial arts after hours: "I left behind my identity as a full professor, an author, and teacher," she explained, "and signed up to study karate."[8] Although there's little obvious connection between martial arts and English composition, she found that "without the monotony of well-known situations," she gained a fresh perspective and self-awareness that she was then able to bring to her day job.

None of this is to say that experience doesn't count. It does. I'm much better at many things than I was 10 or 20 years ago, and I often learn a lot from people who have been working in their fields for a long time. I quote many experts in this book because I respect the wisdom they've gathered over their careers. But I still learn a lot from newcomers, too, and not just because I may have forgotten some basics over the years. The Silicon Valley researchers Mark and Barbara Stefik interviewed dozens of inventors and designers and came to a conclusion similar to Belshee's: that students and others new to a field are able to solve the most difficult problems because they don't know those problems are supposed to be hard and are willing to try "unconventional ideas that an expert might say were silly or illogical."[9] That's why it's often best to have the most diverse set of colleagues you can find. We can learn from both experts and beginners, and ideally remain both experts and beginners ourselves.

All of us act like those closed-minded experts sometimes, and all of us can benefit from a bit more beginner's mind. This is as true at home as it is at work. It's true everywhere in life. Parents can learn from their kids, teachers from their students, and (perhaps especially) bosses from their employees. The great Indian Buddhist teacher Santideva knew this way back in the eighth century. He wrote: "One should be the pupil of everyone all the time."[10]

Zen master Dogen was a bit more grandiose in his wording. As he put it, "A beginner's wholehearted practice of the Way is exactly the totality of original enlightenment." In simpler terms, the path to awakening is to approach your whole life with beginner's mind. Awakening doesn't mean knowing everything. It's much closer to knowing nothing.

CHAPTER 8

Working without Working

AS WE DISCUSSED IN THE LAST CHAPTER, ONE RISK OF getting too narrowly focused is to lose our beginner's mind. Yet we usually think the best way—maybe the only way—to get ahead in our jobs is to work harder and harder. Stories abound of people working ever-longer hours, even taking on multiple shifts or multiple jobs, all to get ahead.

But what if the answer is to work less?

About 20 years ago, researchers at the University of Connecticut ran an experiment at two local insurance companies. They asked desk workers there to take four breaks every hour: three for just 30 seconds and then one for three full minutes. In other words, participants were asked to pause every 15 minutes for at least a quick breather, and to take a more substantial break each hour. All this was in addition to the longer breaks (such as for lunch) already built into their daily schedules.

Did all these extra breaks slow things down? On the contrary, the ones taking the breaks seemed to get more done! The researchers called this "empirical support for the utility of frequent, short rest breaks."[1] Workers can be more productive when they aren't *always* working.

It's easy to get sucked into the cult of busyness. We don't feel productive—we don't feel useful—unless we're *doing* something, and preferably more than one thing. We *want* to be busy. We're slightly embarrassed if we don't *look* busy. Even when we're not working at our jobs, we have to be accomplishing *something*. We set goals for our exercise routines and hobbies, and even for our meditation practice. When friends ask us how we're doing, we often answer proudly, "Busy!"

As we'll discuss in a later chapter, goals themselves are not necessarily bad. But there is also real value in taking a break every now and then. Certain kinds of thinking require not just conscious effort but also periods of unconscious "incubation." Many historic discoveries happened while famous "thinkers" were not actually thinking, and even creative endeavors seem to be aided by periods of rest.* In more technical terms, "Creative discoveries result from a process whereby initial conscious thought is followed by a period during which one refrains from task-related conscious thought."[2]

Taking breaks at work isn't lazy—it's essential. It's not just our creativity that needs time to take shape. Our bodies and mind are simply not made to work nonstop. We need time to recover, and we can't do that without a break. Study after study has shown that taking breaks doesn't reduce productivity, and often increases it.[3] A study of telemarketers in Korea found that those who engaged in relaxing, social breaks during the day had better sales.[4] A study of factory workers

* Paul McCartney claims to have written the melody to "Yesterday" in a dream.

on an assembly line in Europe found that "frequent short breaks" improved attention levels throughout the day—and we've already talked about the importance of paying attention![5] There are even benefits to that most notorious office time-waster: surfing the internet. Contrary to popular belief, a recent study found that what researchers euphemistically called "workplace internet leisure browsing" is actually "an unobtrusive interruption which enables restoration of mental capacity and fosters feelings of autonomy."[6] So go ahead and check your Facebook.

This may sound obvious, but working on something else doesn't count as a break. Research shows that breaks are only effective if you actually stop working. (Who would have thought?) As one review of the science notes, "Employees who engaged in work activities, such as preparing work materials for their next meeting, during breaks experienced more negative emotions later."[7] If you're filling out an expense report or a time card, sweeping the floors, or rinsing some dishes, you're not taking a break. This is just switching up your work tasks, and it's not bad, but remember: "It is precisely [the] absence of work-related demands that allows for the process of recovery from work to occur."

The key to a successful break is true detachment. Perhaps for this reason, using your smartphone on a break seems to be counterproductive. A survey of 450 office workers found that the ones who got on their phones on their breaks reported significantly more "emotional exhaustion," and didn't seem to reap the usual recovery benefits when they got back to work.[8] Why would smartphones be bad if web browsing is good? It may come down to what these activities are replacing. When you're sitting at your desk, a little recreational internet might be a welcome break from work-related tasks. But when you're actually trying to take a break, your phone can suck you back into the messages and emails waiting for you.

In addition to giving yourself time to rest, it's also important to give yourself time to think. Back when I worked as a software engineer, I had a boss who would get upset whenever he saw us sitting at our desks and not typing. I tried to explain once that we also needed time to think—to solve difficult coding problems or design the software itself. "Do that in your car on the way home," he answered. "No thinking at work." This is obviously terrible advice. I had another boss in those days who himself spent *a whole week* every year away from the office doing nothing but thinking. Guess which of these two was more successful?

If your job hasn't been automated, it's probably because it requires real thought. Trust me. Make time every day for thinking.

Of course, we don't just need breaks during the workday. We need a break after work as well. There are lots of reasons for this, including that there's more to life than our jobs—or there should be! (We have a chapter on finding the right balance coming soon.) But even from the narrow perspective of job performance, endless hours at the office can become counterproductive. A long-term study in Great Britain found that "long working hours may have a negative effect on cognitive performance."[9] Men and women who worked more than 55 hours per week scored lower on a cognitive reasoning test than those who worked 40 hours a week. Furthermore, "Long working hours predicted decline in performance on the reasoning test over a 5-year follow-up period," suggesting that those who worked more also deteriorated more over time.

Of course, deliberately working less goes against the grain of many corporate cultures. Researchers analyzing one large global consulting firm found that workers who were *perceived* as working long hours were labeled as more successful and were more likely to be rewarded and promoted—even if they were only pretending to embrace their firm's excessive work culture.[10] Managers seemed unable to distinguish between those who actually worked long hours and those who didn't, as long as the workers didn't reveal their shorter hours explicitly. If you don't make a big deal about your breaks or your saner quitting time, your boss may not even notice.

I knew a manager once who made a rule never to describe himself as "busy" because he didn't want his staff to think that busyness was the goal. If you're a manager yourself, try to model taking real breaks, both throughout the day and after work. I try not to message anybody after hours, even if I find myself working, so employees and colleagues know it's OK to disconnect. Give yourself permission to do this, too. An unenlightened boss may get annoyed from time to time when you don't respond at all hours, but in the long run your work will only improve from the extra time to rest.

The great modern Vietnamese Zen master Thich Nhat Hanh illustrates the power of not-working with the metaphor of a glass of muddy water.[11] No matter how much you shake it up, the glass will never get clear. In fact, the more you move it, the cloudier it becomes because all that movement just stirs up the mud. But if you leave the glass alone, if you don't *do* anything to it at all, the mud gradually settles to the bottom and the water clears. From stillness, comes clarity.

Or as the futurist and historian Alex Pang writes: "Rest is not idleness. It is the key to a better life."[12]

CHAPTER 9

Buddha on the Bus

WAY BACK IN THE 1950s, A DOCTOR AT ENGLAND'S MED-
ical Research Council noticed something interesting about
employees of the London transport system. Looking at the
health records of 31,000 employees on those iconic double-
decker buses, he found that the drivers had much higher
rates of coronary heart disease than the conductors working
the same shifts.[1] In most other respects, the two groups were
largely similar: same ages, genders, lifestyles. But the drivers
spent all day sitting, while the conductors spent the day on
their feet—and that made all the difference.

We tend to think of Buddha as a sedentary soul, sitting
alone, contemplating the universe. And he did sit and meditate, of course, as we've already discussed. But the truth is,
he spent *a lot* of time on his feet. He crisscrossed several
kingdoms spreading his teaching, almost constantly on the
move. In fact, the eventual rules he established for monks
and nuns strictly forbade those followers from spending too
much time in one place. You might imagine that the proper
role for Buddha on a bus would be as the driver, leading
the way, but he actually lived his life much more like the

conductors, shuffling up and down the aisles, tirelessly ministering to every passenger onboard.

At one time, work for all of us usually meant physical activity, whether at a factory or on a farm or in a shop. But many of us today spend our working days sitting still, a bit like that imaginary image of the Buddha—but at a desk rather than on a mountaintop. By one recent estimate, employees today spend 62 percent of their workday sitting.[2] We've become a nation of bus drivers, with the poor health to prove it.

You probably don't need me to tell you that exercise is good for you, but the deleterious effects of a sedentary life and work go way beyond our hearts. As best as we can tell, physical inactivity is "an actual contributing cause to at least 35 unhealthy conditions, including the majority of the 10 leading causes of death in the U.S."[3] In terms of the global impact on life expectancy and death from noncommunicable disease, the health risks of physical inactivity appear roughly comparable to the risks from obesity and smoking![4]

There is also good evidence that exercise improves more than your physical health. Regular physical activity also works wonders on your mental state, reducing both stress and depression,[5] and it seems specifically to improve our mind-set at work.[6] Exercise even improves our thinking. A single bout of exercise measurably improves cognition, and these results hold true regardless of age.[7] It doesn't have to be a sweaty session of Cross-Fit, either. A series of experiments at Stanford University found that even just walking "opens up the free flow of ideas,... increasing creativity and increasing physical activity" at the same time.[8] (I try to take a walk at work as often as I can.) The Stanford researchers found that walking outside was best, but that even walking on a treadmill helped stimulate creativity.

These positive effects on our minds might be part of why exercise seems to improve our productivity at work, too. One study of several hundred hospital workers in Seattle, Minneapolis, and Denver found that even moderate exercise significantly improved work performance.[9] A similar study of 201 adults in Southwest England found that "exercise improved mood and performance, leading to better concentration, work-based relationships and heightened resilience to stress."[10]

If we know that exercise is good for both our health and our productivity, does that make sitting bad? The answer seems to be a bit complicated. For one thing, jobs that require a lot of sitting often pay better than jobs that require us to move around. Peek into any office building, and you'll probably see well-compensated executives and middle managers parked in meetings and minimum-wage janitors and security guards on their feet. Because those higher-paid workers can afford better health care, this can mask the negative health effects of all that sitting.[11]

That said, a survey of over 200,000 adults in Australia found that "people who sit the most and perform no weekly physical activity" had "the highest all-cause mortality"—meaning they literally died earlier than their less sedentary neighbors.[12] In fact, this study estimated that "sitting was responsible for 6.9% of all deaths" among these adults aged 45 and older. And about 25 percent of those adults sat at least eight hours per day.

Knowing how important it is to keep moving, would an office-bound Buddha use a standing or treadmill desk? There is some evidence of health benefits to these approaches to exercise at work, but I remain skeptical. The Mayo Clinic in Minnesota found that volunteers who worked at treadmill desks did get more physical activity than those at traditional workstations, and that there was some increase in employee performance.[13] But that was only after an initial *decrease* in performance, presumably because it is actually difficult to walk and work at the same time. Earlier research by the same team found only "very small" impacts on employee health from treadmill use, and no increase in supervisor-rated performance, again after an initial decline.[14] A comprehensive survey of 23 studies of standing and treadmill desks found that typing and mouse performance was decreased on treadmills, resulting in reduced productivity.[15]

As we'll discuss later, Buddha was not a big fan of multitasking. A day at a standing or treadmill desk might be better than a day of unrelenting sitting, but better still would be a day spent alternating sitting with an occasional walk or other physical activity. This may sound like an unimaginable luxury, but with a bit of planning, these walks can often be incorporated into your workday. I once had a job that involved lots of one-on-one meetings with various coworkers, and I convinced almost all of them that we should do these while walking around the building. I would routinely rack up 10 miles of walking on heavy meeting days! At another job, we were in a somewhat crowded space with no obvious place to walk, but I managed to find another floor of the building that was still under construction and would walk there with my colleagues, doing long loops through the empty halls. At other times, I've held walking meetings in the parking lot. Most of us find walking-and-talking more natural than treadmill-based forms of walking-while-working. I certainly do.

There seems to be a nice synergy between mindfulness and exercise, too. When researchers from the University of Louisville surveyed members of a local YMCA, they found that those with stronger mindfulness were better able to stick to an exercise regimen.[16] They concluded that perhaps something about the "non-judgmental, present-focused awareness" developed through mindfulness training helped prevent the all-too-common exercise "relapse," where our good intentions fall to the wayside after a few weeks (or less!). Researchers attempting to use mindfulness to help dieters noticed the same thing: Women who attended mindfulness workshops found themselves exercising about three times more per week six months later.[17] It seems that practicing mindfulness encourages us to stay active—perhaps from building a stronger awareness of our own body and its needs. When researchers in Eugene, Oregon tried to recruit volunteers to compare long-time meditators who exercised with those who didn't, they couldn't find *any* sedentary meditators at all![18] As the researchers explained: "All meditation practitioners reported habitual participation in moderate exercise of some kind."

At the same time, exercise seems to improve our mindfulness, just as mindfulness improves our exercise. A study in Finland found that "physically active adults had better mindfulness skills compared to less physically active adults."[19] And as we discussed in chapter 5, mindfulness has health benefits of its own, similar and complementary to those of exercise. This may help explain why Japanese Zen monks—who spend countless hours sitting more perfectly still than the most dedicated office worker—nevertheless appear to have better-than-average overall health.[20]

Finding a way to take an exercise break during the workday has multiple benefits beyond the purely physical. First, it creates natural pauses in your day—and we just discussed the importance of taking breaks in the last chapter. Second, breaking up long sedentary periods at work with even light exercise seems to help offset the impact of all that sitting.[21]

Third, if you can find a way to exercise with your colleagues, that seems to come with added benefits, too. When three hospitals in Denmark instituted a workplace exercise program, they found that workers who exercised with their colleagues had more energy and experienced fewer aches and pains after work.[22]

How much should you exercise? That answer will be different for each of us. There is risk from overexertion, from too much exercise, as well as too little. Buddha's advice would be to avoid either extreme. As a recent international study concluded, "Moderate exercise appears to be the sweet spot," if your goal is to increase health and longevity.[23] Frequent high-intensity training can be counterproductive—but don't let this become an excuse for an entirely sedentary life. As the Indian Buddhist sage Santideva warned: "The more the body is protected, the more fragile it becomes, the more it degenerates."[24] Pushing yourself a little is a good thing.

For most of us, research suggests that something more like "a short, leisurely jog a few times per week is adequate."[25] Pretty much any exercise seems to help! A study in Canada found that even employees who just biked to work were less stressed than those who drove.[26]

My own routine is to run a mile, first thing in the morning. I'm not a particularly fast runner, so this takes a little over 10 minutes, including warming up a bit at first. I charted out a one-mile loop through my neighborhood, so I can get up, get dressed, and get this quick bout of exercise in before my first cup of tea—or my first email. It's not a lot, but I can tell it makes a difference to my mental and physical health.

Buddha made time every day for physical activity, and you should, too. The bottom line is that it's essential to take care of the human body. Our physical form is precious. That monk Santideva also wrote that "The body is like an object on loan."[27] Everything we do in this life—working, playing, loving, even meditating—is done with this body. And the best way to care for it is to live life like those London bus conductors—and like Buddha himself. You have to keep moving.

Physical activity is essential to your physical health, your mental health, and your productivity at work. Find a form of exercise that works for you. Commit to it regularly. Do something active at work every day, even if it's just a walk around the office or around the block. Your body will thank you, your mind will thank you, and, eventually, your boss will thank you, too.

CHAPTER 10

Sleeping to Wake Up

BUDDHA LIVED BEFORE SMARTPHONES, COMPUTERS, television, radio, electric lights—even before books and magazines. Anything you wanted to do after sunset had to be done by lamplight, and lamp oil was expensive. It seems safe to assume that life after dark was pretty dull. There was little to do between dusk and dawn except sleep.

Perhaps for this reason, Buddha worried a lot more about his disciples sleeping *too much* than sleeping *too little*. In one lecture to laypeople, we find this verse:

> *Sleeping late, adultery,*
> *Picking quarrels, doing harm,*
> *Evil friends, and stinginess,*
> *These six things destroy a man.*[1]

Believe it or not, that wasn't even the worst of it. Elsewhere he got still more judgy, complaining about "the sluggish and gluttonous simpleton who sleeps and rolls around like a fat, grain-fed hog."[2] Ouch!

These days, things are pretty different. With so many distractions at our fingertips, it's undersleeping—not oversleeping—that's become an epidemic. In her book, *The Sleep Revolution*, the best-selling author Arianna Huffington describes her own literal collapse from chronic lack of sleep, her body and mind so wrecked that she recalls fainting and hitting her head, "coming back to consciousness in a pool of blood."[3] For most of us, the proverbial wake-up call may not be so dramatic, but her story of living on three or four hours of sleep, fueled by near-constant infusions of coffee, will likely ring true for many. About 6 percent of the US population reports getting less than five hours of sleep on a typical weeknight, and about 40 percent report getting less than six hours. Such short sleep has been associated with everything from obesity and diabetes to increased risk of heart disease, cancer death, and even suicide.[4] Even if we avoid the most extreme pitfalls, lack of sleep can still leave us overweight and unhappy.*

All this sleeplessness comes at a real cost in the workplace. We may think we're being heroes by squeezing in an extra hour of emails and reports when we should be in bed, but the opposite is a lot more likely. A review of recent research into insomnia found that it is "consistently associated with excess absenteeism" at work, as well as higher risk of accidents and reduced productivity. Instead of turning us into office superstars, lack of sleep can "inhibit career progression" and "degrade

* *Buddha's Diet,* my first book (co-written with Tara Cottrell), has a whole chapter on how sleepless nights make us fat.

job satisfaction."[5] One study found that the average US worker loses the equivalent of 7.8 days of productivity each year due to lack of sleep, which costs their employers roughly $2,280 per employee.[6] Another study put "fatigue-related" drops in productivity at $3,156 per employee for insomniacs—more than twice that of employees who got good sleep.[7] And it isn't just the cost to companies. A recent economic analysis found that a one-hour *increase* in sleep "increases earnings by 1.1% in the short run and 5% in the long run," even though sleeping more leaves less time for actual working.[8] That's a *lot* of money—and it doesn't even count the savings to your monthly Starbucks bill.

The cure for all of this is simple, but not easy: more sleep. So how do you get it?

You need to start by making sleep a priority. You should be as worried about being "late to sleep" as you are about being late to work—maybe even more so, since losing that sleep will mess up your work the next day, too. Decide when you need to wake up in the morning, and subtract eight hours from that. That's the *latest* you should be getting to bed, because that's when you should *already* be asleep.

Create a bedtime ritual. Some people find it helps to read, ideally on actual paper (see more on this on the next page). Others may prefer to write in a journal or have a cup of herbal or decaffeinated tea. Stay away from alcohol as a sleep aid, though. While a drink or two may help you fall asleep, it also disrupts your sleep[9] (among other problems).

Don't eat late at night and try to get some exercise during the day (as we just discussed). Both of those help a lot.

There are a few more nonnegotiables. First, perhaps the most important thing you can do is stop using your phone and other electronic devices at night. About 90 percent of Americans use some electronic device in the hour before bed,[10] with "interactive" devices like smartphones and laptops causing the most sleep disruption. Seemingly innocuous e-books and e-readers can be problematic, too. Studies have shown that when people used these devices, they typically "took longer to fall asleep and had reduced evening sleepiness" as well as "reduced next-morning alertness," compared to when they read a printed book.[11] Even the dim light of such devices suppresses the hormone melatonin, disrupting the natural sleep cycles. There is no substitute for just shutting off your devices well before it's time to go to sleep. Trust me.

Second, you need darkness. Put simply, your brain is programmed to sleep in the dark and wake up in the light, and fighting this natural tendency can wreak havoc on your circadian clock. A survey of recent studies found that nighttime exposure to bright light causes all sorts of sleep problems.[12] Start lowering the lights well before your intended bedtime, and if you can't get your bedroom truly dark (or you sleep with a partner who still stays up late), invest a few dollars in a decent sleep mask. You'll be amazed at how much of a difference this makes.

If you simply can't get enough sleep at night, brief naps

during the day are another option. Napping has long been associated with laziness, but this stigma is thankfully starting to fade. There is good evidence that even a short nap can make us more productive,[13] and can improve subsequent job performance.[14] The key is to find a quiet place, and not to sleep *too* long. Most people find 15 to 30 minutes sufficient. That sleep mask we just talked about can come in very handy here, too.

By the way, even Buddha had to deal with nap-shaming. There's a story that one of his monks once criticized him for taking a nap, saying that some *other* teachers called this sort of behavior "abiding in delusion."[15] This was apparently quite an insult among ancient Indian masters and not one Buddha took lightly. Buddha explained that it was a hot day and he had just eaten—and anyway what mattered was who was enlightened and not who took a nap. (And, by the way, Buddha was enlightened and the monk wasn't, so abide in that, buddy.)

Buddha considered restful sleep one of the many benefits of meditation. In one story, he explains: "The peaceful one sleeps well, having attained peace of mind."[16] Elsewhere he elaborates that after the "liberation of the mind" through meditation, "one sleeps well, one awakens happily, [and] one does not have bad dreams,"[17] among many other pluses—including becoming pleasing to other humans, which also sounds pretty good.

Modern meditators often find this, too. One clinical study found that patients in a six-week mindfulness meditation curriculum not only improved their sleep but also had fewer symptoms of depression and fatigue.[18] Others similarly find significant improvements to "insomnia and sleep disturbance" from mindfulness-based treatments.[19]

Whether or not you want to meditate just before you go to bed is up to you. Some people find that it clears their mind and helps prepare them to sleep. But other people get up from meditation feeling more alert and awake. For them, mornings are a better bet. Traditional Buddhist monasteries typically do both, with organized meditation sessions first thing in the morning and last thing before lights out.

What if you're lying in bed, in the dark, you've avoided eating late, you stayed away from alcohol or caffeine, you exercised that day, and you still can't fall asleep? Even if you don't do formal sitting meditation in the evenings, some of the same techniques we talked about earlier can often help you relax. Find a comfortable position in your bed, and gradually relax every muscle, starting with your toes and working your way up to the crown of your head. Then listen to your breath, trying your best not to focus on anything else. Watch your thoughts come and go without letting yourself get sucked in. Leave your phone where it is, even if you suddenly remember a text you meant to send. Remind yourself that nothing is more important right now than letting go and getting to sleep.

It will take some experimentation to find a routine that works for you. Don't stop trying. Sleep is one of the greatest gifts you can give yourself. You'll work better and feel better. Just remember, you can't wake up without first going to sleep.

CHAPTER 11

Telling the Truth

MANY FAITHS HAVE AN INJUNCTION AGAINST LYING. In the Old Testament, not lying is one of God's Ten Commandments (either eighth or ninth, depending on who's counting).* Islam similarly considers lying a grave sin. Buddhism is no exception. Buddha insisted that any monk who told a deliberate lie had to confess his misstatement.[1] Elsewhere, he includes lying with killing, stealing, and adultery as something to be avoided by all of us—monks, nuns, and laity alike.[2]

But you don't need me or Buddha to tell you not to lie in general, and not to lie on the job in particular. You already know that. And yet much of the time we don't tell the truth at work—especially in difficult situations. One study suggested that the average adult lies at least once a day![3] And the tendency to lie at work may be even greater than in other social settings.[4] We hedge or dodge tough questions. We give vacuous answers and tepid feedback instead of speaking our true mind. We nod in fake agreement when our boss says something crazy. Why?

The popular author and co-founder of Radical Candor, LLC Kim Scott suggests that this is how we've been taught throughout

---

* It's generally eighth for Catholics and Lutherans; ninth for Jews, Orthodox Christians, Calvinists, and Anglicans. The Bible doesn't number them clearly.

our careers to "avoid conflict or embarrassment."[5] We think the key to job success is getting along with everyone, not rocking the boat, and that doing this means avoiding hard truths. Yet, in fact, Scott explains, the results of being honest are often much more positive than we imagine, even when we're delivering a tough message: "You fear people will become angry or vindictive; instead they are usually *grateful* for the chance to talk it through." In the end, no one actually likes being lied to.

But there's nuance to being honest, and Buddha understood that, too. Just because something is true doesn't mean it's the right thing to say right now. This is something I never managed to explain to my grandmother. She couldn't resist sharing what she *really* thought about my choices—whether in sweaters or careers. I've had countless colleagues who never understood it, either. They'd take every opportunity to belittle their coworkers, pointing out each harmless mistake in the name of candid feedback. But being honest doesn't have to mean being a jerk.

Buddha talked a lot about what constitutes "right speech," which he believed to be an integral part of the path to nirvana. Truth was just a piece of it. Before saying anything, even if it's true, Buddha suggests that we ask ourselves a few more questions: Is it helpful? Is now the right time? And is it kind?[6]

Let's talk about helpful first. If a colleague shows up to work wearing hideous shoes, you are under no obligation to point this out. If an incompetent coworker is fired, you do not need to say, "I'm surprised you lasted this long." The question is not *just* whether these statements are true, but *also* whether they are what the other person needs to hear. You need to ask yourself if hearing these things will help them in any way.

Most of us have a limited ability to absorb criticism. If you're asked for feedback on a presentation or report that's a complete disaster, it's often most helpful to choose one or two places where your colleague can improve the most and save the rest of your feedback for the next round. If a coworker asks for feedback, it's often best to clarify up front what exactly they are looking for from you. If they just want a high-level thumbs-up or thumbs-down, they may not appreciate a line-by-line markup of their grammar and style.

Similarly, nothing can get done in a workplace if we are endlessly debating the same questions over and over again. One thing I like to remind myself is that if I'm working with a group of smart and well-intentioned people, the second-best decision is almost as good as the best one.* So even if I'm *sure* I'm right about something, at a certain point, it's best to set aside my disagreement so the team can move on. Once it's clear that further discussion isn't changing anyone else's mind, it's not helpful to continue voicing my dissent.

Buddha also worried about the *when* as well as the what. As alluded to above, if a team is struggling with a particularly

---

* If I'm *not* working with a group of smart and well-intentioned people, it may be time to move on anyway. If you can't trust that the second-best decision will usually be a good one, you may have deeper misgivings about this team or this work that need to be addressed.

contentious question, it may be time to keep further misgivings to yourself. Many people also respond poorly to public criticism, so a big group meeting may be the wrong time to offer feedback on their work, no matter how well intentioned. When someone has just gotten a thrashing from their boss, it may be the wrong time to admit that you mostly agree. When someone has just given a high-pressure presentation to a big client, it may be the wrong time to tell him how badly you thought it went. They'll figure that out soon enough, and you can always bring it up later if they don't.

I'm sure you can think of countless other examples. Saying even the right thing at the wrong time is often much worse than saying nothing at all—especially when we know the truth is going to be difficult to hear. That's why Buddha considered finding the right time to give feedback as important as speaking the truth. As he put it:

> "The one I consider most excellent and sublime is the one who speaks dispraise of someone who deserves dispraise, and the dispraise is accurate, truthful, and timely; and who also speaks praise of someone who deserves praise, and the praise is accurate, truthful, and timely."[7]

In other words, whether we're sharing praise or dispraise, timeliness is key.

Buddha's last admonition on "right speech" is perhaps the hardest, but also indispensable: You have to be kind. This is not to say that everything needs to be sugarcoated, but even the most direct criticism can be "spoken gently," as Buddha put it, "with a mind of loving-kindness."[8]

The most important thing to remember is to show care for the person and save criticism for the work. No matter how bad a job someone might be doing, they are a human being, worthy of your respect. You need to make this respect clear to them in *all* your interactions, not just when you're expressing criticism. You build up trust with colleagues by caring for them every day—asking about their partners or children, checking in after an illness or tragedy, inquiring about a recent vacation. Colleagues want to be seen as whole people, and will be much more receptive to criticism if they know it comes from a sincere desire to help.

The same is true when we're on the receiving end of such feedback. Try to accept criticism as a reflection of your work, not your self, even if your criticizing coworker is not skilled in making that distinction. And whether you agree with the feedback or not, don't let the discussion become personal. Buddha advised us not to hate the people who criticize us, no matter how harshly. He asks us not even to hate someone who might "sever you savagely limb by limb with a two-handled saw"[9]—which it can feel like sometimes when our work is under attack.*

* In case of actual limb severing, though, you should definitely notify someone in HR.

Another thing to keep in mind is that, for most of us, it's much harder to be cruel face-to-face than it is by email or text or phone. This means it's much safer to deliver criticism in person. I had a boss years ago who instructed me never to say anything negative to anyone by email—advice I routinely forget, and then instantly wish I had remembered. Not only is our own tone hard to judge when we communicate electronically, but we lose all the subtle signals of how our feedback is being received. When we're physically present, we can usually sense what the other person is hearing, and not just what we think we're saying. We can modulate our tone and adjust our phrasing if we sense something isn't landing as we intended.

These lessons on kindness are particularly tricky if you're a manager or supervisor, because then it's your *job* is to give honest feedback. Many managers try too hard to be kind, resulting in what author Kim Scott calls "ruinous empathy," which she says, "is responsible for the vast majority of management mistakes" she sees in the corporate world.[10] The primary goal of giving feedback at work isn't generally to make someone feel better;* it's to help them work better. Delivered well, honest feedback can often accomplish both. Again, the key is to be direct and focus any criticism on the work, rather than the person. The great Indian Buddhist teacher Santideva summarized Buddha's guidance as follows: "One

---

* There are exceptions to this. I've had people at work tell me they have cancer, that someone close to them is sick or has died, or that a marriage is dissolving painfully. Those situations are the wrong time to offer critical feedback. Offering comfort is the priority; work-related criticism can wait.

should speak confident, measured words, clear in meaning, delighting the mind, pleasing to the ear, soft and slow, and stemming from compassion."[11] If you can deliver *that* kind of feedback, you're on your way to being a *very* good manager.

To be clear, Buddha didn't consider any of these questions a license to lie. The traditional monastic codes provide for *very* few exceptions to the no-lying rule. Buddha allowed that sometimes we speak too "hurriedly" and thus make a mistake.[12] He made another exception when we simply misspeak, saying one thing when we mean another. In both cases, we should correct the mistake when we can, but it's not considered a violation of Buddha's rules. But that's about all the wiggle room Buddha allows. In a lecture he gave to his own son, he says, "I will not utter a falsehood even as a joke."*[13] Yikes!

Buddha offered all these considerations mostly to encourage us to think before speaking at all. Remember, less is very often more. Buddha was a big fan of silence, and of knowing when to pause. Like so much advice in this book, the best path is one of deliberation and balance. Think before you speak, choosing the right time and place as well as the right words. As Buddha put it in another verse: "Bettetr than a thousand meaningless statements is one meaningful word, which, having been heard, brings peace."[14]

---

* Buddha was not a great dad, as we'll explain in chapter 17. But his son was eventually ordained as a monk and joined Buddha's sangha, after which Buddha did his best to train him.

CHAPTER 12

Bickering Buddhas

GIVEN HIS LOVE OF TRUTH TELLING, YOU MAY BE SURPRISED to learn that Buddha worried a lot about arguing. One of the gravest offenses in his monastic code was "causing a schism" in the sangha—basically letting arguments get out of hand. He had likely seen this doom other schools of yoga and meditation around India in his day and didn't want his followers falling into the same trap. He also understood that any group of people spending lots of time together are bound to have disagreements—*especially* when they commit to telling the truth, as Buddha insisted his followers do. When he listed the five "grave deeds" that lead to an immediate rebirth in hell, letting arguments get so out of hand that they created such a schism was right up there with *killing your mother.*[1] He thought it was that bad.

So Buddha knew that finding healthy ways to disagree would be essential to his community's survival. His monks and nuns would have to learn to argue constructively and resolve disputes amicably. This is just as true in the workplace as it is in a monastery. A certain amount of conflict on the job may be inevitable, but unchecked it can get out of hand. Disputes there may start with seemingly minor "task conflicts," essentially disagreements on how some piece of work is supposed to be completed. But things get messy when those morph into "relationship conflicts"—in other words, when things get personal.[2]

Buddha's advice to his monks contains solid wisdom we can use at work. Most importantly: Fight fair. As Buddha explained, if someone is questioning you about something, it's never the right response to "crush him, ridicule him, and seize upon a slight error." Basically, don't be a bully. Buddha called anyone who resorts to such techniques "unfit to talk."[3] I agree.

It's also essential to focus on ideas, not people. As we just discussed, Buddha placed a high value on truth. It doesn't matter *who's* right—it matters *what's* right. The goal of any debate or argument at work should never be to "win," but to discover the truth.

For this reason, there is no particular value in scoring rhetorical points or exploiting some unintended misstatement. Regardless of the skill of our opponent, we should be arguing against the best possible version of the opposing view. When two people on my team disagree, I sometimes have them try an exercise where they each do their best to summarize the opposing view. Forcing yourself to think through the logic of the other side, and trying to express that position as favorably as you can, often helps reveal where you might find common ground. You might even convince yourself to change your mind!

All this brings us to the topic of meetings. Almost no one looks back on a day at work and thinks, "I wish I'd had more meetings." Yet meetings are a big part of how work gets done in many organizations. And meetings are probably where most workplace arguments end up.

Like so many things in this book, it's possible to have both too many meetings and too few. The problem of too many meetings is obvious: No one has time to *do* all the things that get decided in the meetings. Too many meetings can also trigger a vicious cycle. I once worked at a company where almost everyone was always in meetings. This meant you could never catch anyone at their desks, so the only way to speak to them was to schedule yet another meeting. The meetings multiplied and the problem only got worse.

Too few meetings may sound like a contradiction in terms, but it happens and also causes issues. I worked at a start-up once that had no scheduled meetings at all, and had only a single meeting room for the whole company. One happy result was that we all had lots of unstructured time to do serious, thoughtful work. It was also easy to find specific people when you needed to talk to them. But it was *very* hard to talk to lots of people at once. You could try to corral everyone you needed into an impromptu discussion, but invariably someone would be off doing something else, unaware that they were needed for this particular unscheduled chat. By not planning these discussions in advance (in other words, by not *scheduling a meeting*), we could never be sure we'd get everyone we needed together at once.

Most meetings fall into one of two categories: decision making or information sharing. Decision-making meetings will generally be active discussions involving all (or at least most) of the attendees, while information-sharing meetings are often more passive, with perhaps even just one person talking and the rest listening. Some people will argue that this second category has become obsolete and that email or other electronic means are better for one to-many communications. I don't agree. There is still something unique about hearing directly from a coworker. There is a level of nuance and emotion that can be lost in written communication, or even in streaming videos and the like. In a sense, every lecture the Buddha gave could be considered a meeting of this second sort, and these were so valuable that his disciples memorized what he said!

Meetings can also be both too large and too small. In a decision-making meeting, the risk is usually that the meeting is too large. The rule of thumb is that you should invite all the people needed to make the decision, but no more than that. The reason to be strict here is that the quality of a discussion declines quickly with lots of participants. Two-person conversations are very efficient—each of you can make your points and respond to the other right away. Once you have three people, the back-and-forth is trickier, and it only gets worse from there. The more people involved, the harder it will be to keep things on track.

You can usually tell if a decision-making meeting is too large if some people are not participating, or if the discussion is going around in circles. When you see this happening, it's best to pause and propose a smaller meeting to sort out this particular point, and then move on.

In an information-sharing meeting, the risk is usually that the meeting is too small. Here you want to include *everyone* who needs to know whatever information is being shared. Since it's usually only one or a few people talking anyway, adding more people just adds to the audience and so makes the meeting *more* efficient, not less. In these situations, it pays to be generous with your invitations.

A common problem is getting confused about which sort of meeting you are trying to have, or setting up meetings that are a bit of both. You then have to navigate the conflicting pressures of wanting to make the meeting small and large at the same time. It's sometimes best to split these hybrid meetings in two: a small meeting for making the decisions, and a larger meeting for communicating those decisions to a wider group.

Many people see meeting invitations as a source of status. After all, if decision-making meetings are being kept as small as possible, then being invited to one must mean you are important, even essential. I certainly felt that way for many years. I fought to attend what I thought were the important meetings, and resented the times I wasn't included. This is another reason meetings get too big—we don't want to hurt anyone's feelings by leaving them out. My daughters' preschool teacher had a saying that "There's always room for one more." That's a wonderful spirit of inclusion for playgrounds and parties—and I try to follow it!—but it's terrible for many meetings.

As I've progressed in my career, I've come to feel exactly the opposite way about meeting invitations. Now any meeting I'm excluded from is a small victory. If people are able to make a decision without me, then I have informed and empowered them successfully. I must be doing something right. I only want to be invited to meetings where I am truly required and, even then, I hope to set things up so I won't be required next time.

In recent years, I've also developed a few ground rules for myself in meetings. First, never interrupt anyone who's speaking—or trying to speak. This is much harder than it sounds! Many companies and teams have a culture of interrupting, so that if you wait for a true opening before you speak, you can't speak at all. Even so, I try to make a conscious effort not to interrupt people, and to find other ways to signal that I'd like to speak next. Interrupting people in meetings is highly contagious, but waiting your turn can be surprisingly contagious, too. When you stop interrupting, you'll find that others often stop as well.

Second, in decision-making meetings, I try to ensure that everyone gets to speak and that no one monopolizes the conversation. After all, if the meeting was correctly constructed to begin with, everyone there *needs* to participate—otherwise, they wouldn't have been invited. There should be no pure spectators in a good decision-making meeting.

Yet oftentimes you'll see one or two people dominating the discussion, and several people not speaking at all. Of course, it's possible that the wrong people were invited—in which case you might want to propose that the meeting be rescheduled with a smaller group, as mentioned above. But, more often than not, the issue is that some of the necessary voices are struggling to be heard. I try to encourage the quieter members to speak up. "I don't think we've heard from…" is a good way to create some space for others.

Third, I try to follow the rules of disagreement we discussed at the start of this chapter. The goal of the meeting is to make the right decision, not to feed anyone's ego. It doesn't matter *who* turns out to be right as long as we come to the best conclusion. Debate in meetings should never get personal. No one should leave a meeting feeling personally attacked, and even those on the "losing" side should leave feeling heard.

Finally, we can't become obsessed with perfection. It is often more beneficial to make a *good* decision now than to make the *best* decision later. Again, in a room full of smart, well-intentioned people, even the second-best decision is probably still quite good, and almost certainly good enough.

Meetings, despite their much-derided reputation, can be extremely productive. Buddha's original sangha held meetings twice a month, on new-moon and full-moon days, to recite the monastic rules and confess any recent violations. All monks and nuns attended, and all participated in the discussion.

Most of us probably can't get by at work with just one meeting every two weeks, but we can try to ensure that all the meetings we attend are both necessary and efficient. We can commit ourselves to listening to others, and not getting overly attached to our own views.

I don't know anyone who truly enjoys fighting with their coworkers. I certainly don't. The Buddha believed that all "beings wish to live without hate, hostility, or enmity," that instead "they wish to live in peace."[4] I bet that's how you feel most days.

Any healthy group of dedicated people will include a variety of opinions. Even enlightened people seem to disagree once in a while—as you'll see if you ever attend a meeting of Buddhist masters. Yet you can live in peace even when you disagree with your colleagues. Just remember these basic rules and you'll never let your workplace arguments get out of hand.

CHAPTER 13

How to Be Ambitious

IF THE CAUSE OF ALL OUR SUFFERING IS OUR CONSTANT striving for more, where does that leave our careers? Doesn't a successful job require us to *want* to be successful—specifically, to be *more* successful than we are now? That would seem to require a certain level of striving. Can we truly succeed in business without really trying?

In many respects, Buddhist monks traditionally went all-in on this lack of ambition, and still do in the Theravada sects common in Southeast Asia. They go out each morning to beg for food and are strictly forbidden from saving any food from one day to the next. In a very real sense, they start each day with literally nothing*and hope that all their needs—at least from a nutritional perspective—will be provided by the community. They have no reason to strive for any material possessions beyond their daily needs because they are prohibited from accumulating any wealth. Even extra food donations would simply have to be given away at the end of the day, so begging longer or more effectively

---

* OK, not *literally* nothing. They are allowed three robes, one bowl, a razor, a water-strainer, and a needle and thread.

doesn't accomplish anything useful. More food on any given alms round would just be more to carry—and potentially more to waste.

But that system only works because not *everyone* is or ever was a monk. *Someone* had to be thinking of the future. Someone had to plant and harvest crops according to the seasons. Someone had to plan and prepare meals. Eventually, someone had to earn enough money to donate funds to build monasteries where monks and nuns could live and roads where they could walk.* Buddhists tend to view the arrangement as mutually beneficial, with the monks and nuns spreading the dharma with the laity's support. But regardless of whether or not this seems fair to you, the fact remains that the monks can only live this way because someone else is planning ahead.

And, even beyond that, why does anyone become a monk or a nun in the first place? Clearly not for the money, since monks and nuns are prohibited from even handling money, and also not for any of the other trappings of wealth and power like fancy homes (forbidden) or clothes (forbidden) or sex and drugs (both forbidden). But it seems reasonable to assume that many of them at least are chasing after *something*. It takes effort to leave your home and live under these

---

* When China invaded Tibet in the 1950s and began dismantling their monastic system, the Chinese authorities claimed the Tibetan monks were exploiting the laypeople by living lives of idleness while others worked. The fact that the Tibetan people were willing, even eager, participants in this arrangement was seen as a sign of their brainwashing.

austere rules. There must be *some* motivation behind it. Isn't striving for awakening still a form of striving?

Buddhists have faced this paradox from the beginning. Buddha himself was clear that his years after leaving the palace were not aimless wandering. He had a goal, a purpose. He was searching for something. And eventually he found it. If he had accomplished nothing in those six years, we wouldn't call him the Buddha. He'd be the long-forgotten Prince Siddhartha, just another disappearing deadbeat dad.

Mindfulness itself implies a sort of goal—the goal of bringing our full attention to everything we do. Buddhists are firm believers in the old adage that anything worth doing is worth doing well. You see this attitude at play in Zen temples throughout Japan, where it applies equally to the skilled artisans crafting pottery and paintings and to the silent monks raking sand. There is nothing wrong with trying to do your best work, always, regardless of what you do. And this *trying* is itself a goal.

Buddhists often have long-term goals, too. Big projects take time, whether that's building a new temple or finishing medical school, filling out a complicated spreadsheet or closing a deal. Nothing would get done if none of us had goals. I could never have written this book without goals.

But not all goals are created equal, and not all goals are worthy of our efforts. Later branches of Buddhism considered the bodhisattva vow to be the highest of goals. Bodhisattvas are fully enlightened beings—potential Buddhas—who have nevertheless decided to delay entering complete nirvana until they have freed all other beings from suffering, too. (We'll have a chapter on this goal specifically toward the end.) After that goal, the second most noble goal would be the individual quest to discover our own awakening. If that sounds a little selfish, the traditional reasoning behind elevating such a goal is that we can't truly help other people overcome suffering until we have done it ourselves. Otherwise, we're still inevitably trapped in our own selfish desires—at least now and then. If we truly want to be dedicated to taking care of others, we also have to take care of ourselves.

Where does this leave career goals, like getting that next promotion, landing that next client, or making that next sale? How about angling for a raise or bonus or just applying for a better job?

Buddha taught that *bad* goals, unhealthy or unwholesome goals, tend to stem from three problematic sources: greed, hate, and delusion. Any goals motivated by one of these three is inherently tainted. Conversely, any goal free of such taints might well be just fine.

This can be a little tricky to work out in practice. We often have to look quite deeply at our goals to uncover our true motivations. There might be nothing wrong with wanting a raise so that you can provide security and comfort for your family. But more money alone won't save a failing marriage or nurture neglected children. That requires love, not money, and believing otherwise is simply one of the many delusions that lead us astray.

Similarly, wanting a promotion because you think you could do better work with a bigger team or broader responsibilities, or wanting a new job because you think you would be better suited to it, may be just fine. But treating salaries or titles as a sort of scorecard for life is a manifestation of greed.

And hate is bad, too—but you probably knew that already. Trying to get ahead simply to get even with someone else or to have power over others is never a good goal.

Some longtime meditators end up with the opposite problem—not too many goals, but too few! Once they realize that a fat bank account or an impressive resume won't bring true happiness, how can they stay focused on work at all? What's the point?

At some level, they're right: There is no point. It's no easier to realize awakening in a mansion than in a tiny shack. It may even be harder. Buddha fled his life in the palace for a reason. There was something distracting about all that luxury. But a life of pain and deprivation wasn't the answer, either. All that physical anguish created its own distractions.

As with everything in Buddha's teachings, the answer seems to be about balance, about finding that middle way. Some material success in life can be useful and help provide a foundation for practice. And it's all relative. For some people, taking time off work to join a weeklong meditation retreat sounds like an unimaginable luxury. For others, having to work the other 50-odd weeks instead of living full time at a temple might seem like a terrible hardship. The right balance of work and family and practice will look different for each of us. If you want to quit your job and move to a temple, and you can afford to do that, I certainly won't stop you. But if you want to keep working to support yourself and your practice, there's nothing wrong with that, either. As long as your goals are pure, either path can be noble.

Keep in mind that even the most illustrious goals can sometimes become distractions. There is a famous story about Ananda, one of Buddha's most accomplished disciples. Ananda attended almost every lecture given by Buddha, and his prodigious memory meant he could recite them all word for word. After Buddha died, his disciples decided to assemble 500 of his fully awakened followers so they could agree on his true teachings and ensure that they would propagate them correctly to the next generation of students. Of course, they wanted Ananda there with them. He knew more of the teachings than anyone! But there was a catch—Ananda hadn't realized awakening yet.

Bummer! Ananda was super-upset. The other students agreed to make an exception—the meeting would now be 499 enlightened students plus Ananda. Problem solved! You can imagine how humiliating that sounded to him. Ananda vowed to realize awakening before the meeting. Nothing wrong with that! In theory, that's a perfectly noble goal. The drive to awakening was one of Buddha's goals, too. Yet this extreme focus on the future and not the present got in Ananda's way. And, in this case, there was some basic impurity in Ananda's motivations. He wasn't trying to realize awakening to end suffering or to help others—he just didn't want to be embarrassed at the meeting. It was all about ego, really, a form of greed. And so Ananda meditated as hard as he could, but he still couldn't get there. He was stuck.

The night before the meeting, Ananda knew it was down to the wire. He stayed up all night meditating, just as Buddha had before his own great awakening. No luck. By morning it still wasn't happening. He was out of time. He would have to swallow his pride and attend the meeting as everybody's collective +1. He had failed. He lay down to catch some much-needed sleep, having given up his goal of realizing awakening—and bam! Before his head touched the ground, he had his awakening. All he had needed to do was stop obsessing about the goal.

Sometimes we have to do a task just to do it. We have to take pride in our work and bring our full attention to it. There's nothing wrong with having wholesome goals, as long as we aren't motivated by greed or hate and we're honest with ourselves about what these goals will and won't accomplish. But we can't let the goals themselves become just another distraction. We can't let them stop us from paying attention. Sometimes the best way—even the only way—to achieve our goals is to let them go.

CHAPTER 14

What Yoda Got Wrong

IT'S NOT ENOUGH TO HAVE GOALS. YOU ALSO HAVE TO make an effort. You have to try.

Some people think of Buddha as a happy-go-lucky, anything-goes kind of guy. The chubby smiling statue you see in Chinese restaurants—who is *not* actually the Buddha*— reinforces this stereotype. The Buddhist beads you see draped around hippies and Phish fans contribute to that image, too. Depictions of the true Buddha typically show him sitting or perhaps lying down. He tends to look peaceful and content, dignified, and wise. But he never looks like he's *trying* very hard.

In reality, Buddha was not a go-with-the-flow type at all. He *did* try. He worked hard and expected his followers to work hard, too. He cared a lot about what he called *effort*. Awakening isn't just something that happens, he explained. In order for a monk to follow the path, "he makes an effort, arouses energy, applies his mind, and strives."[1] As the scholar-monk Bhikkhu Bodhi summarizes, "The work of self-cultivation is not easy" and requires "unremitting effort." There is no substitute for

---

* He's a tubby monk from China who became a symbol of good luck. His name is Hotei in Japanese but Budai in Chinese—which may be one source of confusion.

doing the work, and "there is no one who can do it for us but ourselves."[2]

Buddha also worried a lot about laziness, the flip side of effort, perhaps because it is so easy to mistake meditation for idleness. He listed laziness, along with alcoholism and gambling, as sure ways to ruin. He got pretty specific, too, describing these dangers of getting too lazy:

> Thinking: "It's too cold," one does not work; thinking: "It's too hot," one does not work; Thinking: "It's too early," one does not work; thinking. "It's too late," one does not work; Thinking: "I'm too hungry," one does not work; Thinking: "I'm too full," one does not work.[3]

We've probably all had days like that, days when we can find countless reasons to do nothing and not much reason to do anything. And you've probably worked with people who seem to feel that way every day.

In the work arena, we usually call this phenomenon *burnout*, and it is a real problem. As Buddha knew, anything worth doing takes effort, and that includes everything from career advancement to spiritual awakening. You won't get anywhere if you can't summon the energy to try.

The key to avoiding burnout and maintaining effort at work seems to be doing things you enjoy and find personally fulfilling. That may seem both intuitively obvious and occasionally impossible. But the good news is that research in the workplace suggests you don't have to love your job *all* the time. Researchers at the Mayo Clinic surveyed hundreds of doctors on a wide range of topics covering work characteristics and career satisfaction.[4] What they found may surprise you: "Physicians who spent at least 20 percent of their time in the aspect of work that was most meaningful to them had a rate of burnout roughly half that of those who spent less than 20 percent."

That is, spending just 20 percent of your time doing the part of your job you truly love can be enough to keep you motivated. In the Mayo Clinic study, spending more time than that didn't make much of a difference. This was true regardless of which parts of the job those doctors loved. Some found the greatest fulfillment in caring for patients, some in teaching other doctors, and some in running the administrative side of things. But it didn't matter *what* they found most meaningful, as long as they spent at least 20 percent of their time doing it.

In a typical eight-hour day, 20 percent is a bit more than an hour and a half. It's not *that* much time. One approach is to make this the first thing you do when you get to work. Another is to make it a reward for getting other tasks done. I've tried both and find both strategies effective. Sometimes it's more a matter of pausing to realize that you're *already* doing the part of your job that brings you meaning. Maybe you're working in retail or the service industry, and what you really love is talking to customers and helping them find whatever they need. That may not be something you can schedule in advance, but you can remind yourself each day that this is what makes your job special.

I have two other rituals that help me find this balance. First, when I get to work, I make a list of things to do that day. Some of these will be things I need to do, but others will be things I want to do. Writing all these down helps a lot, both so I don't forget anything and to keep me motivated throughout the day. Second, before I go home in the evening, I try to look back on my day. How did I spend my time? What did I accomplish? Did I get to the parts of my job I love?

You can use these rituals to help make sure that you're spending some time each day on the things you find most rewarding. Start by including a few of these on your list—they are just as important in the long run as that new project your boss gave you or that deadline looming this week. Writing these down along with your other daily priorities ensures they won't get lost in the hectic rush of other work.

At the end of the day, look back on how you've spent your time. Do you feel good about your choices today? Did you spend at least an hour or two doing work you love? If not, what changes can you make tomorrow to get yourself back on track? Try to make tomorrow a little more balanced than today.

A lot of the other techniques in this book can also help keep your energy up—like eating well, getting enough sleep, and exercising regularly. When you find your energy flagging badly, try to take a break and walk around, even for just five minutes. If you can get outside, even better—our bodies and mind are trained to wake up in the sunlight.

Another contributor to burnout is failure—or just *fear* of failure. It's hard to keep up your energy when work isn't going well. Working on a project that fails feels like a waste of time.

But it *isn't* a waste of time. Failure is a useful signal—it tells you you're taking real risks. If you never fail at anything, you can't be trying anything very hard. In Silicon Valley, entrepreneurs often talk about the virtue of "failing fast."[5] This is not to say that failure is good necessarily, but if you are going to fail, better sooner than later.

Applying this to your own work, it's often useful to tackle the hardest part of a risky project first. If you fail, at least you haven't invested too much time yet. You can move on to the next thing. If you start with the easy bits, you could end up working weeks or months on something before you find out your approach isn't going to work after all. By starting with the most challenging parts, you also get the excitement of discovery, the thrill of tackling the unknown. This often helps keep you motivated. Even if it doesn't work out, you'll learn a lot working on something difficult. And if you succeed, you can forge ahead to the end knowing it should be mostly smooth sailing.

For most of us, effort and ambition often go hand in hand. You can't accomplish anything without effort, and it's easier to maintain your effort when you have a goal in mind. Your daily to-do list encompasses your short-term goals, while your career ambitions describe your long-term goals. You don't want to obsess about these on a daily basis, but reflecting on your career progression monthly or so can help keep you motivated day by day. When you realize that one of your goals isn't going to work out, you cross it off and reorient yourself toward another one. You always keep trying.

There is a story that Buddha was once residing at a monastery with hundreds of his most devoted followers. After a brief visit to a nearby village, many of the monks sat around making small talk instead of meditating.[6] Buddha saw them lounging around idly and admonished them for not trying hard enough: "It's up to you to make strong effort, teachers only tell you how."[7]

Once again, goals in themselves are not enough. You have to work hard. The universe's most famous fictional Zen master is probably Yoda, the diminutive teacher who instructs Luke Skywalker in the *Star Wars* movie series. Yoda famously told Luke, "Do or do not. There is no try."[8] Sadly, on this particular point, Master Yoda got it wrong.

CHAPTER 15

Remembering to Breathe

LET'S SAY YOU'RE DOING EVERYTHING WE'VE TALKED about so far. You're meditating. You're paying attention. You sleep well and eat well and exercise frequently. You tell the truth and argue honestly. You have wholesome goals and make a healthy effort to achieve them.

And you're still having a bad day at work.

This happens. I have bad days. You have bad days. Even the most experienced meditators I know have bad days.

Oftentimes, bad days come down to some sort of misunderstanding, what Buddha would call a delusion. One of Buddha's lessons was that things are not always what they seem. Our mind plays tricks on us. Sometimes our mind makes things look better than they really are. At work, I think the mind usually makes things look worse.

In my job, I try to distinguish between two kinds of problems, which I call real problems and fake problems. A real problem, quite simply, is one that, if not solved, will cause something bad to happen. A fake problem, on the other hand, is one that you can ignore without any real negative consequences.

This may sound like an obvious distinction, but once you start trying to categorize problems at work this way, it's amazing how many problems turn out to be fake. For example, a common problem for many people on the job is the hunch that a colleague or boss doesn't like you. That never feels good, and often causes us a lot of stress. It *feels* like a problem that needs to be solved. But ask yourself: What happens if you *don't* solve it? Unless this alleged dislike is causing actual conflict and interfering with your ability to do your work, you can probably just ignore it. You don't need everybody to like you, even if that might feel good.

At larger companies, you'll sometimes hear concerns over things like two people having the same or very similar titles or two teams have the same or very similar missions. This can create tension, and sometimes leaves both sides feeling threatened, even if they rarely get in each other's way. Another common issue is two different ways of doing a certain task, or disagreement over the right format for some sort of meeting or report. Surely consistency is better, right? Perhaps. But faced with such a situation, I often ask myself what will happen if I don't do anything about it at all. Quite often, the answer is nothing.

People bringing fake problems to me at work will often underscore their urgency by explaining how long the problem has persisted—perhaps weeks or months or even years!—not realizing that this is evidence of the *absence* of any real problem. If a situation has existed for months or years without negative consequences, it's probably not a real problem. And if the only consequence of not solving the problem is that it will still exist a month or even a year from now, that's yet more reason to doubt that we have to solve it. A problem that gets no worse in a year is probably not much of a problem.

This philosophy admittedly runs counter to the famous aphorism, "Never put off until tomorrow what you can do today." It is perhaps closer to Mark Twain's farcical version, "Never put off till tomorrow what you can do day after tomorrow just as well."[1] This is not to endorse laziness, which we just discussed in the previous chapter. Work that needs to be done should be done and should not be unnecessarily delayed. But many of us spend our days at work faced with more problems than we can realistically solve. That is a common source of these bad days. In such a situation, it makes sense to focus on the ones that matter.

To be clear, there is nothing *wrong* with solving fake problems per se. Sometimes it's worth solving such problems just so people will stop talking about them. (This counts as a consequence, albeit a fairly small one.) It's just that your effort should be proportional to the benefits. If people are wasting lots of time worrying about a fake problem, it's worth a *small* effort to resolve it. But you wouldn't want to devote lots of time to something just to pacify the worrywarts.

In other words, it's not that fake problems aren't problems

at all. *Someone* presumably thinks they are real. But you do not need to be that someone. It's a little like the old Zen saying: "Things are not what they seem. Nor are they otherwise."[2] Fake problems are still problems, but they don't have to be *your* problems.

Still, there will be some days when all the real problems feel like more than you can possibly handle. Sometimes it feels like *everything* is on your shoulders—and no one else is doing anything at all!

When this happens to me, I try to ask whether I've brought this on myself. Why have so many projects landed in my lap? Oftentimes, I realize that it's because I asked for them! Maybe I didn't believe that anyone else could handle them. Or worse, I was *sure* other people could do them, and I was worried that my boss might realize that I wasn't needed!

I have a few remedies for this. First, trust your colleagues. Don't feel that you have to do everything. It's very rare in most companies to have a job that only one person can possibly do. For one thing, it's a huge risk. What if you're sick? Or move away? Who will do the work then? The sooner someone else learns the ropes, the better for everyone.

Second, don't fight for work. If someone else wants to take over a task, I almost always let them. There are *very* few things that I feel I have to be the one to do. There is almost always more than enough work to go around. A lot more. Try not to get territorial, and accept help when it's offered.

Third, admit your limitations. Don't try to hide when you have too much to do. Tell your boss. Tell your colleagues. The worst thing you can do is exude confidence right up until the deadline, and then let everybody down. If you need help, ask for it—as soon as possible.

And when all else fails, don't forget to breathe.

We've already discussed breathing in the context of mindfulness meditation, and you can also use breathing throughout the day as way of overcoming moments of stress and despair. As the Vietnamese Zen master Thich Nhat Hanh put it, "Breathing is a means of awakening and maintaining full attention."[3] It is a tool we carry with us constantly, available every minute of the day. "Breath is essential to our existence,"[4] the renowned yoga teacher Eddie Stern explains, and "the link between the breath and the spirit is at the root of nearly every single contemplative and religious practice."[5]

Buddha agreed. He taught that we could achieve full awakening just through awareness of breathing. There's a story that Buddha was completing a three-month retreat with some of his best students when he decided that they still could make even more progress on their path to awakening. He told them that he would stay an extra month to give them additional instruction. Word of this got around, and even more monks and nuns gathered to hear this monthlong bonus class from the Buddha. And what Buddha taught that month was the technique he called full awareness of breathing.

Whole books have been written on breathing meditation,[6] but a fairly simple version often works wonders on tough days at work. Start by taking a deep breath wherever you are. Try to feel the air enter your nose or mouth. Feel it fill your lungs. Feel your chest rise and then fall. Feel the air returned to the wide world.

That's all you have to do.

I find that three mindful breaths like this are often enough to calm me down most days. Now I can go back to whatever I was working on before. On a really bad day, I might need to do this several times—perhaps even every hour. Luckily, that's easy enough. A minute or two is all it takes. You can even set an alarm to remind yourself to do this throughout the day as needed.

Notice what your "normal" breathing is like on tough days like this. Oftentimes, it's short and clipped. After a few of these mindful breaths, your breathing should become a bit more relaxed again. Your whole body starts to relax.

Awareness of our breathing brings "great fruit and great benefit," according to Buddha.[7] I can't promise that breathing alone will turn your bad day at work into complete nirvana. But I can promise that it will help. You might try to make this a part of your routine on every day, good or bad. But on our bad days, it's especially important to remember to breathe.

PART 3:

HINDRANCES

CHAPTER 16

Attachment and Detachment

AS WE'VE DISCUSSED, MOST OF BUDDHA'S LECTURES were recalled by just one guy: his close disciple Ananda. Ananda possessed considerable powers of memorization and recited the vast majority of Buddha's known teachings to the 499 other enlightened students who had gathered at the First Council after Buddha's death.

But it turns out that Ananda missed a few things. Among Buddha's other great disciples was a woman named Khujjuttara, who worked as a palace slave for one of the many royal families of ancient India. She overheard the Buddha once while running errands in the local village and became a devoted student. She would return to hear him preach as often as she could and then repeated his teachings to the Queen and other women at the court. Her recounted lectures always began with the same phrase, "This was said."[1]

Khujjuttara ultimately outlived her Queen and experienced enlightenment herself. When the Buddhist scriptures were compiled, her recollections were added to those of Ananda's in a separate book, titled *Itivuttaka*, the Pali word for that repeated phrase: *This was said*.

So what exactly did Khujjuttara recall? What *had* the Buddha said in that village? *Itivuttaka* covers a lot of topics, but one of my favorite lines is a simple one. When describing the most important factors in our path to awakening, Buddha explained: "I do not perceive another single factor so helpful as good friendship."[2]

In other words, even awakening is easier with friends.

Two of my best friends today I met at my very first full-time job during a summer in college. I've found other dear friends through work in the decades since. On the other hand, many of the friendships I formed at various jobs over the years have not survived the inevitable transitions from company to company—or even team to team within the same building. And not all work relationships are positive to begin with. The dreaded "office politics" haunts many companies. At times I've left a job with lingering resentments toward some of my former coworkers, even if it's now hard to recall exactly what I resented. This continuous process of relationships good and bad, forming and fading, is woven into the fabric of modern working life.

Many of us spend long hours at our jobs, surrounded by other people, and it's natural to form close relationships. For many, the personal bonds we forge at work are much of what give our jobs meaning. I don't need to like *everyone* I work with, but if I don't like *anyone* at a new job, I'm unlikely to last long. And I'm not alone—studies of workplace friendships find that having friends at work significantly reduces employee turnover.[3] Our colleagues often bind us to the job as much as our salaries.

These workplace friendships don't just make work more fun. As Buddha taught, these friendships are an important source of support. One recent study found that "positive relationships at work are energizing, both physically and emotionally,"[4] impacting not just our productivity, but also our physical health. Almost everything about work is better if you like the people there.

Not everyone treats their work friends the same way. Men and women, for example, seem to avail themselves of workplace friendships somewhat differently. In one New Zealand study, women seemed to derive "more social and emotional support from their friends," while men treated their work friendships as more "functional" relationships.[5] But friends are generally considered important to employees of all genders.

Yet there can be some downsides to workplace friendships. Perhaps the most obvious is simple distraction. Almost by definition, a work friendship extends beyond the practical requirements of your job, and there are times when the burden of supporting a friend can be a significant drain on your focus.[6] We've probably all had the experience of a friend who wants to unload about a relationship crisis or a family problem when we'd really like to get ahead of our next deadline.

Employee friendships can also become exclusionary and

create barriers to other employees. The dreaded "old boys' networks," still seen in many companies and industries, are the most famous manifestations of this darker side to workplace camaraderie.[7] And while positive working relationships can bring great joy and fulfillment, negative relationships with coworkers often yield the polar opposite. One research team found that "corrosive work relationships are like black holes that deplete psychological resources."[8]

Like so much of what we discuss in this book, the key is to pay attention and make conscious choices. Find relationships at work that feel supportive and nurture these friendships. Notice the relationships that feel toxic and try your best to remove yourself from them. If your workplace friends are a big part of what's keeping you at a job, make sure they're healthy friendships. And remember that forming new bonds with new colleagues is an inevitable part of most careers.

No discussion of work and relationships would be complete without at least mentioning the issue of *romantic* relationships. I know many happy couples who met at work, but dating colleagues is fraught, to say the least. When you have a falling-out with a partner you meet online or in some purely social setting, you generally have the option never to see or hear from them again. When it happens at work, you might continue to run into each other every day. You might have to work together on a project or a shift. One of you might end up being the other's supervisor down the road. You can't necessarily cut off contact, no matter how bad things get—and they can't, either. This can cause serious problems in a professional setting, potentially ending up with someone getting transferred or even fired. Sadly, historically, things are more likely to end badly for a woman than a man.[9]

On top of that risk, there is also the long history of unwanted romantic advances at work, primarily (though not exclusively) directed at women. According to one study by two researchers at the Cornell University, "Women were much more likely to report having been pursued by someone they were not interested in than men."[10] They also found that, regardless of gender, suitors *greatly* underestimated how difficult it was for their targets to say no. Workplace dynamics are complicated, and a proposal that might be easy to bat away at a party or a bar can feel like a burden or a trap at the office. In part due to these *very* frequent misunderstandings, the researchers found "the line between romantic courtship and sexual harassment is not always clear."[11] And you do not ever want to find yourself on the wrong side of that line.

So if you feel you must make romantic overtures to a colleague, please tread carefully. Ask *once*, and be *very* clear what you're asking. A workplace lunch or coffee is not a date and not any indication of romantic interest. An ambiguous suggestion to meet outside work to discuss a work-related project or problem won't do anyone any good, either. If you must ask someone out whom you work with, just ask them out, with no workplace strings attached.

The most important rule is this: You must take no for an answer. This is easier said than done, but there is no room for romantic persistence at work. For the avoidance of doubt, you should take anything other than a clear yes as a no. Remember, saying no to a colleague is *hard*—probably much harder than you think. Please don't make them do it twice. If you've followed my advice so far, you've made your interest clear. If your colleague changes their mind one day and realizes how perfect you two are for each other, I promise they will let you know. *

It is far safer to cultivate workplace friendships than workplace romances—and, Buddha would say, more fulfilling in the long run. In one of the lectures Ananda *did* remember, he told the Buddha that half of the holy life came down to "good friendship, good companionship, good comradeship."[12]

"Not so, Ananda," Buddha replied. That wasn't quite right. "It is the *entire* holy life."

* I realize that this advice would undermine the plot of virtually every workplace romantic comedy. You should follow it anyway.

CHAPTER 17

Balancing Better Than Buddha

BY MODERN STANDARDS, BUDDHA WAS EVEN WORSE AT relationships and parenting than he was at holding a job. At least he never *tried* working life. But he did try marriage and fatherhood, and failed pretty spectacularly at both, abandoning his wife and infant child to follow his spiritual pursuits.

Buddha avoided the modern question of what is usually called "work-life balance" by renouncing work and home life both. And he did this for a very simple reason: He felt it was easier. You might think monastic life sounds difficult, but to Buddha it was simpler than trying to juggle so many disparate demands. As one scholar summarizes, Buddha understood "the difficulties that anyone in the midst of everyday worries would encounter on the path of inner progress."[1] As Buddha put it himself, "home life is confinement," while monastic life "is like an open space."[2]

But this is one place where I'd encourage you to set your sights higher than Buddha. You can do better.

From the very beginning of Buddhism, not everyone felt

willing or able to follow Buddha's example in this regard. Many of the mothers and fathers, husbands and wives he taught did not want to abandon their families the way he did. For them, as for most of us, finding some semblance of balance was a necessity. Abandonment was not an option.

Balancing time between work and home life isn't easy. It involves difficult choices. In my experience, the only way to make it work is to accept these choices, perhaps even embrace them, rather than trying to avoid them as Buddha did.

I don't like framing this as finding "work-life balance," because it suggests a dichotomy between work and life that doesn't really exist. Work is a part of life—and life has many parts that need to be balanced. In addition to our careers and our personal lives, there's sleep and wakefulness, activity and rest, friends and family, social connection and solitude. Balancing the time we spend in and out of work is only one of many trade-offs we have to make—and not necessarily the hardest or the most important.

These trade-offs can be difficult because life is short and how we spend our time makes a difference. Back in college, my friend Bill and I both got interested in Go, a board game a little like chess that was developed in China and spread to Korea and Japan. We both bought books about it and played a few games together. But Bill got very serious about the game very quickly. He found a professional-level player in town and began taking weekly lessons. He played in tournaments and even traveled to Japan to study the game. I didn't do any of those things. These days Bill probably plays more games in a typical week than I've ever played in my life. And now, 30-odd years after we both discovered the game, Bill is approaching master level, while I remain firmly a novice. I don't know if Bill is a more naturally talented Go player than I am—it didn't seem that way when we were starting out—but he put in *a lot* more time than I did, and that made all the difference.

Much of the challenge of balancing work and home life is that our careers can be a lot like learning Go. How far we advance is in part a result of how many hours we put in—at least up to a point. There are diminishing returns sometimes (more on that soon), but there are often real costs to spending less time working and more time doing other things, including raising a family.

I've had both a job and a family for most of my adult life. When my kids were babies, I took the first shift with them every morning. This meant I was up as early as 4:00 a.m., seven days a week. Once they were fed and dressed, I'd sometimes take them to a neighborhood bagel shop to keep the house quiet, and I knew which of these opened at 6 a.m., which at 6:30, and which not until 7:00. This schedule had a real impact on my work. I stopped working at home, mostly because I couldn't—when I was home, my life there needed my full attention. I never worked late at night because I was too tired after such a long day. When my kids got older and started school, I would drop them off every morning at 9:00 a.m. before going to work and was home by 6:00 p.m. to join the family for dinner. I would deviate from that schedule if I had to go out of town, but that's about it. This also affected my work. If someone wanted to schedule a meeting at 8:30 a.m. or even 5:30 p.m., I politely declined. I'd be surprised if I made many more than 10 exceptions to that rule in 10 years. And if there was a school play or a classroom birthday party in the middle of the day, I left work for that, too.

When I look back, these self-imposed limitations on my professional life had a real cost. As I mentioned above, how much we accomplish at work is partly a function of how many hours we put in, and I put in fewer hours than some people around me. Some of those meetings I missed were important, and my absences had consequences. But in the end I was mostly able to compensate in other ways, and I have no real complaints with how my career has progressed. I'm sure I made many mistakes along the way, but by and large the trade-offs I made worked for me. I think I'm probably not as successful in material terms as I could have been if I had spent more time in the office. But I feel I'm successful enough.

Now my kids are both teenagers. One of them has left home for college. They don't need—and certainly don't want—nearly as much attention as before. This gives me more time to do other things on evenings and weekends—including personal projects (like this book!), but also sometimes a few sundry work tasks. These days I find my Fridays are less stressful if I know I can catch up a bit on Saturday or Sunday. And I have more time to think on the weekend than when I'm trying to squeeze in one last email between meetings or before heading home, and that helps. It's easier for me to get in the office early now or stay late, too. Overall, I'm just much more flexible about when and where I work than I used to be when my kids were younger, and this has probably helped accelerate my career over the last few years.

These problems are sometimes portrayed as primarily affecting women, and especially mothers, but I haven't found that to be true. Recent research backs up my experience. Professor Erin Reid of the Boston University School of Management found that "problems with demands for work devotion are neither only a mother's issue nor only a women's issue," and that, in fact, most workers experience such conflict.[3] We all know at some level that there's more to life than working, and everyone I know struggles to find the right balance.

There are no easy answers. The times I've personally been happiest with the balance were when I loved my work life and I loved my home life and couldn't get enough of either. The times I was least satisfied were when one or the other wasn't going particularly well. I am quite sure the choices I've made now or in the past wouldn't be exactly right for anyone else. And I imagine that my own balance will continue to evolve in the years to come.

As we discussed in the chapter on taking breaks, working nonstop is not even good for our jobs. Our body and mind are like batteries, and they become depleted during the workday.[4] We need to detach in order to restore ourselves and do our best work the next day. As one study found, "continued thinking about work when being at home has a clear drawback" in that it hinders our recovery from all that work stress.[5]

There are also diminishing returns to working longer and longer hours each day. It can even become detrimental to both your productivity and your health. Once, early in my career, I worked for 40 hours nonstop to prepare for an important trade show and effectively passed out. This wasn't good for anyone. Yet within reason, working more can mean accomplishing more, and those accomplishments are often rewarded.

My advice is to make conscious choices. The likelihood that you'll work out the perfect balance may be low, but the likelihood that you'll stumble on it by pure chance is probably zero. I've also found it helpful to pay attention to the choices people around you are making—not to judge them, but to ask yourself what those choices would mean for you. I've learned from others' examples, and still do. I see that many successful people have deep and fulfilling lives outside of work, filled with interests and experiences and relationships that they invest in heavily and greatly enjoy. That's encouraging to me, and I hope to you.

Healthy balance seems easier if you are pretty happy with the rest of your life choices outside of work. If you love what you're doing at work and love the time you're spending at home, then you'll naturally want to get this balance right. Your incentives are all aligned. If you're miserable and begrudge the time spent on one side or the other, it's much harder to think clearly about the trade-offs. Sometimes I've found it easier to focus on being as happy as possible in both places, rather than on getting the split exactly right.

We should also remember that searching for and finding this balance is a blessing—and a privilege. For much of human history, working was a matter of subsistence and survival. We often had little choice in the matter. That's still true today for many in entry-level and lower-status jobs.[6] If you're able to exercise control over when and how much you're working, you're already one of the lucky ones.

Yet how much time you devote to the various activities you care about in life will never be an easy choice. But try to make it *your* choice. Decide what's important to you and devote yourself accordingly. Try not to let your job—or anybody else—make this choice for you.

This advice applies to more than just work. As we discussed in the very first chapter, Buddha described many blessings in life, things that "bring well-being and happiness to all the world."[7] Among these were lifelong learning, spending time with friends, finding a home, supporting a family, helping others, and, yes, working in an honest occupation.

Sometimes the challenge of balancing work and family time, in particular, is presented as an issue of fairness. It seems *wrong* that someone who spends time raising a family should be less successful at work than someone who doesn't. It feels unfair. And it *is* unfair, in a way. It's also unfair that the person who doesn't spend time with their family *doesn't spend time with their family*. That person is missing out on countless rich and meaningful experiences, and that family is missing out on someone who could be a vital and cherished part of their lives.

In the end, we have a limited time on this earth within which to pursue all our passions: not only work and family, but also exercise and sleep, hobbies and other interests, and our spiritual practice. We can't do everything, since whenever we spend time on one thing, we are not spending it on something else. Juggling everything well requires not just deliberate choices but also conscious trade-offs. But that doesn't mean we can't do a lot, and can't find the resulting mix satisfying and fulfilling. It's up to us to make each moment count.

A fundamental text of the Soto Zen school of Buddhism, called the *Sandokai*, or "Merging of Difference and Unity," ends with this simple exhortation: "Do not waste time."[8] That is probably the best advice of all.

CHAPTER 18

You Are Not Your Job

YOU MIGHT WANT TO SIT DOWN FOR THIS NEXT CHAPTER because I have some news that may be difficult for you to hear. Among Buddha's many insights is one that might sound a little crazy.

You don't exist.

To be clear, Buddha didn't mean that nothing exists. He wasn't saying that the whole world is a dream or an illusion. He wasn't claiming that we're all living in The Matrix. He meant something a little more subtle than that.

The physical body most people call *you* is real. If a basketball is hurled toward your head, it will bounce off and not pass right through. It's just that this body isn't really *yours*. Neither is anything else. And if there's nothing that really belongs to *you*, then maybe there's no *you* at all.

Imagine that you have a car and you replace one of the wheels. You'd probably say it's still your car. What if you replace all four wheels? It probably stills feels like your car. But what if, overnight, someone replaced every single part of your car with parts from another car. Now what makes this car yours? Isn't it more like a new car parked in the same space?

But if this isn't your car any more, when did it stop being that? When the first part was replaced? That can't be right—then we'd be getting a "different" car every time we changed the oil filter. Is it when that last piece was replaced? That can't be right, either—then whichever car got that final piece would have to become ours. And what if it took 10 years to replace every single piece—how could the car magically become someone else's on that last day?

But if the car with new parts is not your car, and we can't point to any specific moment when it stopped being your car, then it must have never really been your car to begin with. The concept of "your car" is just that—a concept, an idea. It's not *real* in the deepest sense. In reality, there is no essential thing that constitutes your car. A Zen Buddhist would say your car is *empty*—meaning not that it has no passengers, but that there is no essential thing within it that makes it yours.

Now reflect back on yourself five or ten years ago—or even longer if you're old enough. Maybe you haven't literally replaced any major parts (although maybe you have!), but your body still isn't what it used to be. Individual cells have come and gone. The very atoms that make up the physical matter of your flesh and bones have been swapped with other atoms. Your thoughts are different, too. Your memories are different. Your personality is probably also different. Let's hope you've become more mature over the years. Perhaps you've also become more patient. Or perhaps less patient—that happens sometimes. Maybe you're happier. Maybe you're angrier. But one thing is certain—you're not the same.

Now we're faced with the same dilemma as with that car. If so many parts of you have changed, in what sense are you the same *you?* And if you're not the same you any more, maybe you were never quite *you* to begin with.

This is the essential paradox Buddha discovered—that people are "empty" in the same way as cars.* Everything about us is changing all the time. And how could anything that is so subject to change constitute our essential self?[1] Yet if there is no one unchanging thing that defines our true self, maybe there is no self at all.

So when Buddha says you don't exist, he doesn't mean your body doesn't exist or your mind doesn't exist. They do. He just means that if you examine them closely, there's no *you* inside. And every time you look at them, you'll see something a little bit different.

Let's bring this back to the working world. Many of us feel defined by our work, by our careers. We define other people that way, too. The first thing we ask when we meet someone is often, "What do you do?" And yet our jobs are constantly changing, like parts of a car or cells in our body. Is anyone *really* doing the same job they did ten years ago? Five years

---

* Buddha didn't know about cars, of course. But because he preached that all things were empty, he would have included cars, too.

ago? Even one year ago? How could they? The world changes so fast. Customers change. Competitors change. Technology changes. Laws and regulations change. Whole companies, whole industries, come and go. Is *anything* really the same?

The honest answer to "What do you do?" would be different every year, maybe every single day. Yet how could something that changes so often possibly define us?

Maybe you don't quite accept Buddha's teaching that there's no *you* at all. That's OK—it's a strange and difficult concept, to be sure. But even if you're confident that there's an essential *you* that is constant across all the inevitable changes—all those swapping of parts—it can't have anything to do with your work. You could lose your job tomorrow. You could quit. Your company could go under. Your boss could go crazy. These things happen! They've happened to me. If whatever constitutes *you* can survive years and years of physical and mental change, it can't possibly depend on who issues your paycheck.

You are not your job. Whatever *you* are—you're definitely not that.

And if you aren't your job, then your colleagues are not *their* jobs, either. This is important to keep in mind when we find ourselves arguing at work. Right now this coworker may seem like just another obstacle to getting done whatever you are trying to do. But however frustrating or incompetent they may seem right now, that's not the real them. They aren't defined by their work any more than you are.

This is part of why we can never let work disputes become personal.* Every colleague is as much a whole person as you are. Even if you know each other pretty well, you probably have no idea what's really going on inside them right now. The person on the other side of this argument may have just lost a lover or a friend. They may be caring for a sick child or parent. Or they may just have forgotten to take a lunch break. Whatever is going on, you can be sure it is more than you see. Their life is as complicated and messy as yours, and this workplace is just a small piece of that patchwork tapestry.

When we define ourselves by our jobs, we invite all manner of suffering. We set ourselves up for countless disappointments when things go wrong at work. We start holding on too tightly to our jobs, living in fear of ever letting them go. The Buddha taught that the roots of suffering are not just obvious things like greed and hate, but also delusions. And this delusion that we *are* what we *do* is an especially dangerous one.

If we are not our jobs, what about all our other identities? Buddhists have wrestled with this question for a long time—and still do. As the Zen master angel Kyodo williams has written, Buddha's proclamation that "Every human being, irrespective of caste, race, creed, or birth has within them the potential for waking up," remains a truly radical ethos.[2] Awakening is in many ways the levelest of playing

---

* Another reason is that it just doesn't work very well. People are much more likely to compromise if you are criticizing their ideas than if you are criticizing their whole being.

fields. Yet our inherent oneness, our basic human common-ality, doesn't erase our differences. We each carry to work a unique history of suffering—suffering that for many is bound up within the categories of race, sexuality, and gender. Zen master Zenju Earthlyn Manuel explains that "oneness" does not mean "sameness."[3] The fact that all cars are empty doesn't make Hondas the same as Fords. We, too, have differences.

The workplace has never been equally accessible to every-one—and the Buddhist sangha has also struggled to be truly inclusive. The emptiness of self does not change this bitter truth. Yet the realization that we are not our jobs can create space for all our other identities to flourish. It helps us see those who work with us for who they truly are. It lets us acknowledge and address all dimensions of human suffering. If you belong to a historically marginalized group, your job does not replace that identity. You bring that identity with you and have as much right to be at work as anyone else. If you are among the historically privileged, you can commit yourself to welcoming and cherishing your colleagues in the full embodiment of their being. This is the heart of Buddha's radical message—that all things are possible regardless of our form.

CHAPTER 19

Dealing with Distractions

THE WORLD IS A DISTRACTING PLACE. AND WHILE IT HAS certainly become more and more distracting in many ways, this is not a new problem by any means. As the futurist and best-selling author Alex Pang writes in his masterful book *The Distraction Addiction*, "Humans have always had to deal with distraction and lack of focus—and for thousands of years, they have been cultivating techniques that effectively address them."[1]

Let me confess something at the outset: I am *very* easily distracted. If I sit at a restaurant with a television, I can't help watching it. If I hear someone talking at the next table, I lose track of my own conversation. If I pick up my phone to check the time, I might not put it down for 10 minutes.

In other words, focus does not come easily to me. I have to work at it. Years ago, I used to take my laptop with me to meetings, thinking I was being efficient by checking email during the slow parts. Then I realized I was paying no attention to the people around me, sometimes forgetting to get up when the meeting was over. Now I leave my computer at my desk—and try to keep my phone in my pocket.

Smartphones are, of course, a huge source of distraction. Studies find that their use "increases reaction time, reduces focus, and lowers performance" of anything requiring concentration.[2] This is why, by one estimate, smartphone distraction now contributes to almost a quarter of all traffic accidents.[3]

The problem is that we are far, far worse at multitasking than we think. No matter what we tell ourselves, "Only a limited amount of information can be attended to at any given moment."[4] We may think we're expertly juggling half a dozen tasks at once, but we're really just switching between them very inefficiently, repeatedly disrupting our concentration.

Buddha placed great value on concentration, and much of his teaching on meditation describes how to get into the deeper and deeper states of concentration that he called "absorptions."[5] But you don't have to be an experienced contemplative or yogi to understand the value. We've all had the experience of being fully absorbed in some activity. In popular psychology, this total absorption is usually called "flow," and can be defined as that "subjective state that people report when they are completely involved in something to the point of forgetting time, fatigue, and everything else but the activity itself."[6] It can be an exhilarating experience—as well as an extremely productive one. But it is very fragile.

Distraction is the enemy of flow. The mere ringing of a cell phone—not yours, but someone else's—is sufficient to measurably disrupt concentration. In one study, classroom students whose lecture was interrupted by a ringing phone performed worse on a pop quiz than those listening to the same lecture without interruption.[7]

Multitasking is essentially a form of intentional distraction. Switching between multiple tasks disrupts our working memory, an effect that only gets worse as we get older.[8] In one study in Canada, students who used a laptop during a lecture scored lower on a later test—perhaps not a huge surprise. But even those students without a laptop who just sat near the ones on their screens were so distracted that they scored 17 percent lower, too.[9] As the great Indian Buddhist monk Santideva put it, a distracted mind "is not fit for any work."[10]

So what do we do about all these distractions? Meditation helps. People tend to think of the goal of meditation as clearing your mind and calming down, but that's not the whole story. Meditation is really about what happens when we stop meditating. A big part of why we practice mindfulness in a quiet room away from distractions is so we can draw on that skill when we're in a noisy office surrounded by chattering coworkers. Bringing our full attention to focus on our breath in meditation strengthens our ability to concentrate in daily life, in the same way that lifting weights in the gym strengthens our muscles and allows us to lift heavy things elsewhere.

You can also make things easier on yourself by cutting down on unnecessary distractions whenever possible. Put down your phone—preferably in a place where you can't see it. Schedule your time checking email or Twitter so you're not clicking over there constantly. Close unnecessary windows on your computer. Go fully offline even. There are apps that will track your online time and even kick you off the local network during certain hours—try those if you need to. Maybe get away from your desk if people are prone to interrupt you there. Give yourself permission to spend extended time   an hour or more—disconnected and focused on a specific task.

Those who work at home face special challenges of distraction because your whole life is surrounding you as you try to work. If you can, create a space that is just for working—even if you have to set it up and take it down each day. If you're working at the kitchen table, *only* work there—sit somewhere else to have lunch so that you're not tempted to work and eat at the same time. (More on that in the next chapter!) Try to keep your work tasks and home tasks separate, and schedule time for each. When it's time to start work, stop doing the dishes or straightening up the living room, just as you would if you had to rush out the door. If you have others at home while you're working, especially kids, it's even more important to try to create some separate space for yourself—and, of course, even more difficult. Be honest with yourself about what you can accomplish, and don't torture yourself by trying to do many things at once when your home life demands your attention.

There is such a thing as good multitasking.[11] Because we

can't shut our ears the way we can shut our eyes, our brains seem to have evolved to deal with noise distractions differently than visual distraction. That's why many people actually find it easier to work with music playing, for example. (My daughter used to claim she could study better with the TV on in the background, but she would really only listen to it, not watch it.) I myself can't seem to work with headphones, but many of my colleagues swear by them and wear them to listen to music much of the day. I often like to have conversations with colleagues while walking, which I find allows me to concentrate better on what they are saying than if we were just sitting alone in a room. To quote Alex Pang once more, "These kinds of multitasking encourage flow," rather than disrupt it.[12]

In the end, you have to find patterns that work for you. When I'm writing, I like to have all my books scattered around me, an arrangement that looks chaotic and distracting to many people. (I have six books opened within arm's reach right now.) That's how I concentrate best. I prefer working in silence for most tasks, but I love music or a good podcast while I'm doing the dishes or driving. In meetings, I try as hard as I can not to pick up my phone—because I know that, once I start checking it, my concentration is shot.

Your patterns of concentration will be different. Learn them. Pay attention to your attention—when you have it and when you don't. Notice the things that encourage and disrupt your flow throughout the day. Try not to switch repeatedly between tasks.

The modern Zen master Shunryu Suzuki once said to his American students, "You have a saying, 'to kill two birds with one stone,' but our way is to kill just one bird with one stone."[13] I don't want you to kill any birds, but I think you'll find yourself much more productive if you focus on one stone at a time.

CHAPTER 20

Begging for Lunch

BUDDHA CONSIDERED FOOD AN ESSENTIAL SUSTENANCE of life,[1] and I agree. Few things are as important to your health as how and what you eat. I cowrote a whole book on eating based on Buddha's rules for monks and nuns.* Countless others have written their own books on eating, dieting, and nutrition.

But if I had to make just one rule for food and work, it would be this: Please do not eat at your desk.

Believe it or not, Buddha was much more concerned with *how* and *when* his students ate than *what* they ate. Many today assumed that Buddha was a vegetarian, but he was not. His philosophy was basically that beggars can't be choosers, so he ate whatever the local villagers offered him each day.

But one thing Buddha didn't do was multitask his meals.

Sadly, taking a real lunch break at work is increasingly becoming a rarity. In 2016, the *New York Times* estimated that 62 percent of American professionals ate lunch at their desks.[2] You should not be one of them. I say this not because it's messy and unsanitary, although it is. A University of

---

* *Buddha's Diet,* written with my friend Tara Cottrell.

Arizona study found flu viruses on 47 percent of desktops,[3] more than in most bathrooms. You might literally be better off eating from the toilet seat. These same researchers found desktop germs to be a major contributor to the spread of contagious disease.[4] Eating at your desk is definitely gross, but I'm not worried about gross. That's your prerogative.

When Buddha instructed his followers to eat "with attention focused on the bowl,"[5] it wasn't because he was worried about sanitation. He wanted them to pay attention to what they ate. He wanted us to practice mindful eating, not mindless feeding. He considered meals to be a time for meditation.

Perhaps this sounds like an unimaginable luxury to you. We're so conditioned to multitask that to some the idea of doing nothing but eating for even a few minutes sounds almost lazy. But it's not. We know that taking an occasional break can make you more productive, not less. Lunch is the perfect opportunity to put this into practice.

You don't need to take a full lunch hour necessarily— although I try to do this whenever I can. Thirty minutes is enough time for most of us to eat a meal without wolfing it down, and even 20 will do in a pinch. (I usually block out a full hour for lunch on my daily calendar, knowing I will likely end up using some of that to catch up on other work, leaving me with enough time left over to eat in peace.)

As with other breaks, the key to a truly restorative lunch is to take control of the time yourself. If you enjoy socializing with coworkers, then, by all means, invite someone to join you. If you find workplace small talk draining—and many people do[6]—then find a quiet place to eat on your own. If you can get outside, that's even better.[7] The only rule is that you can't keep working while you're eating.

Buddha didn't preach mindful eating *only* as a useful meditation tool—he also saw it as beneficial to our health. There is a story of an overweight king who visited Buddha after having eaten a literal bucket full of rice and curries, "huffing and puffing" as he approached because he was so overstuffed with food. Buddha took one look at him and recited this verse:

When a man is always mindful,
Knowing moderation in the food he eats,
His ailments then diminish:
He ages slowly, guarding his life.[8]

The king was so impressed with the concept of mindful eating that he hired a young courtier to recite this verse to him before every meal. And, sure enough, by practicing mindful eating, the king became "quite thin," according to the scriptures. As the modern monk-scholar Bhikkhu Anālayo summarizes, "As a result of being regularly reminded of the need to be mindful while eating, the king overcomes his tendency to overeat and gradually loses weight."[9]

I can't promise that just taking a lunch break will solve the world's weight problems, but modern studies have confirmed again and again that mindfulness is a helpful part of any diet.[10] When we pay attention to what we eat, we make better choices about our food. We tend to eat healthier and we tend to eat less.

This advice applies to snacking, too. Resist the temptation to grab a handful of M&Ms when you walk by the receptionist, or to munch on potato chips while you finish a report. If you're hungry between meals, it's fine to eat. But do it deliberately. Take five minutes to sit somewhere and eat those chips. Think about what you're eating. Stop when you're not feeling hungry any more. Eat to sustain your body—not to pass the time.

As long as we're discussing eating at work, we should also mention drinking—specifically, drinking alcohol. Drinking at work has a long and storied history (as any fan of the TV series *Mad Men* can attest), almost all of which is negative (as any fan of *Mad Men* can also attest).

So, no surprise. There is ample evidence that alcohol contributes to lots of issues in the workplace.[11] Almost everything about it seems bad. Drinking at work leads to lower productivity, health issues, and a higher incidence of misbehavior of all sorts. A 14-year-long study in Europe found that those who drink excessively are at higher risk for losing their jobs, thereby "solving" the problem of their workplace drinking but creating lots of other challenges for those individuals and the broader society.[12]

Alcohol is one place where Buddha didn't seem to advocate much of a middle ground. He was against it, plain and simple. He forbade his monks and nuns from drinking any "intoxicating liquors" or indulging in recreational drugs, and strongly discouraged laypeople from the practice as well. He listed six specific dangers of consuming alcohol: "diminishing of wealth, increased quarreling, a whole range of illnesses, ill repute, exposing oneself, and weakening of the intellect."[13] Pretty much all of these can be issues at work—especially at the office Christmas party.*

My advice if you choose to drink is to keep your drinking and working as separate as possible. You can have a glass of wine at an after-hours work function, but anything more than that and anything during the workday itself is asking for trouble. And if you've never had a long period of abstinence in your adult life, consider giving that a try. I gradually stopped drinking in my 30s and found that I was much happier without alcohol in my life. You may be, too.

The most important thing is not to let eating or drinking at work become just another distraction. Lunch is the perfect opportunity to take a break, recharge your physical and mental batteries, and practice mindfulness, if only for a few minutes. Don't let it slip away by gobbling down a sandwich or salad while you try to do a dozen other things.

---

* Seriously, "exposing yourself" actually happens, and it's not pretty.

CHAPTER 21

Who Would Buddha Fire?

MANY IN THE MODERN WORKPLACE WILL ONE DAY FIND themselves managers or supervisors of one form or another. According to data from the Bureau of Labor Statistics, nearly 12 percent of US workers were in "management occupations" in 2017.[1] To put that in perspective, that's considerably more than *all* health-care providers—doctors, dentists, nurses, and the like—combined. It's more people than work in food service or factory production. Perhaps unsurprisingly, the percentage increases as we get older and more experienced: It's over 14 percent for workers older than 45. And the numbers are increasing. Management is one of the modern economy's largest and fastest-growing fields.

Buddha wasn't a boss. He never hired anyone and he never fired anyone. So, whether you're a brand-new supervisor or a seasoned executive, Buddha may not sound like an obvious source of management advice. But Buddha did create the Buddhist sangha, a community of monks and nuns who lived by certain rules, and there are some interesting lessons there for anyone managing today.

It's not entirely clear exactly what the rules were in Buddha's day, but by the time they were fully codified and written down, there were *a lot* of them—by one account, 227 for monks and 311 for nuns.* When we talk about these rules today, it's common to talk about what's allowed and what's forbidden. We might say that monks weren't allowed to lie or steal or eat after noon.† And that's true in a certain sense, but also not quite accurate. *Forbidding* something implies a certain authority. Parents might forbid their children from eating too much candy or staying up too late, which is something they can do because they are *in charge* of these children (sort of). Buddha didn't claim that sort of authority. He wasn't a king or a master whose word was law. He was just a guy explaining how the world worked.

What Buddha did say was that certain actions have certain consequences. This is his principle of "karma," or cause and effect. In his mind, much of this was just natural law. If you drop a ball, it falls to the ground— and it falls whether you happen to believe it will or not. Gravity doesn't require you to accept anyone's authority—it exerts its force on believers and nonbelievers alike. Similarly,

* The different modern schools of Buddhist monastics observe somewhat different rules, but all the "traditional" sects (usually called the Therevadin) have more rules for women than for men. Some claim this was necessary in Buddha's time in order for women to be accepted at all, because full gender equality would have been beyond the pale. In many modern Buddhist schools, men and women observe the same rules and are treated entirely as equals. The San Francisco Zen Center, for example, has had several women serve as abbess in recent years.
† The book I cowrote on eating and health, *Buddha's Diet*, grew out of an investigation of this one odd-sounding rule.

Buddha saw karma as a reflection of natural consequences—of actions and reactions. As Buddha explained, "Speak or act with a corrupted mind, and suffering follows, as the wagon wheel follows the hoof of an ox."[2]

The monastic rules are framed as an extension of this. For monks and nuns, certain actions have certain consequences that they might not have for laypeople. For the most serious infractions, a monk or a nun is expelled from the sangha. Because the original sangha was celibate, sex fell into this category: If you broke your vow of celibacy, you were effectively deciding to leave the sangha. But there are only a handful of these absolute prohibitions among those several hundred rules. (My favorite is the rule against claiming supernatural powers.) For violating the rest of the 200-plus rules, the consequences vary from a sort of "probation" period to a simple public confession.

The whole sangha got together regularly and recited the rules and confessed any missteps. So everybody knew the score. There was no "Why didn't anyone tell me I couldn't claim supernatural powers?" excuse. Even today in traditional monasteries, the rules are laid out clearly, right at the outset, and repeated often.

Contrast this with most workplaces. There may be an official employee handbook, but I'd bet no one reads it. And it usually isn't very specific anyway. The rules are often imprecise, and the consequences of breaking them vague at best.

"Discipline up to and including termination" is a common description of a consequence—a very corporate and unhelpful way of saying pretty much anything could happen.

Buddha's approach was very different. He was specific about which actions had which consequences. And he was consistent. He followed his own rules.

It's probably not possible to follow this model exactly in a modern workplace. Your legal department wouldn't want you to try to enumerate every bad action and every consequence, and HR would probably object to the whole ritual of public confessions on the full moon. But you can get close.

If you're a manager, you can start by setting expectations as clearly as possible. What do you want your employees to do? This is harder than it sounds for many people. If you're not used to being a manager yet, it can feel weird or even rude to give someone direct instructions. I've noticed that some new managers try to phrase their instructions as suggestions: "Maybe you could try this?" Many new bosses often don't want to sound, well, bossy. Some don't bother with instructions at all, convincing themselves that it's more polite or even more empowering to let employees figure things out for themselves.

But ambiguity is rarely empowering. It's usually just confusing.

That doesn't mean you should micromanage. Different employees will need different levels of instruction, and Buddha always suggested that we adapt our methods to our audience. With an experienced carpenter, you might be able to say, "Build a table." With someone brand-new to carpentry, you might have to start with how to select and prepare the wood and even explain the difference between a screw and a nail. But notice that what matters here is what level of detail the employee needs, not what is most comfortable for the boss. Elsewhere in his monastic rules, Buddha prohibits "evasive speech and causing frustration,"[3] and that's exactly what we do when we withhold needed information from employees.

If someone working for you is doing something wrong, let them know. And be frank with them about the consequences if they don't start acting differently. This is probably not an easy conversation, but it is a very necessary one. Again, we owe our employees honesty and clarity.

We sometimes feel reluctant to speak negatively about anyone, even our own employees, out of a desire to be nice. This is understandable and reasonable. As we discussed, Buddha himself taught that it was important to speak "with a mind of loving-kindness."[4] But he also placed great emphasis on honesty, and did not see these two principles in conflict. It's *unkind* to be dishonest to our employees, even with the best of intentions. They deserve honest feedback. If they are not doing well, honest feedback is the only way they can improve.

One advantage of presenting all rules in karmic terms is that there is no moral component. The rules and consequences have nothing to do with anyone's worth as a human being. Buddha never claimed that even the most upright monk was worth more than one about to be disrobed. It's not about that. This is why the Buddhist injunction against killing applies to capital punishment[5]—because every life has value, and that doesn't change by breaking even the most serious rules.

Some people's actions are just incompatible with the monkhood, just as some people's skills or temperament might be unsuited to a particular job. It isn't unkind to let these people go—it can be more like helping someone find new shoes if the ones they're wearing don't fit.

At the same time, it is also important to be honest with ourselves. Where have we failed in this situation? Where can we do better? Rather than focusing exclusively on the faults of others, Buddha asks that you consider "what you yourself have or haven't done."[6]

So who would Buddha fire? He would fire anyone who had committed an action for which firing was the appropriate consequence. He would make sure they understood these consequences at the outset, and that they knew what actions had caused them. And he wouldn't make them feel bad about their transgression or misstep, or make them feel they were any less for it. He would wish them well, treating them with kindness and respect at every step.

CHAPTER 22

Walking Away

BACK IN 2013, ECONOMIST AND *FREAKONOMICS* COAUTHOR Steve Levitt launched an audacious experiment.[1] He asked people who were struggling with a life decision to register online and allow him to make the decision for them based on a coin toss.* By the end of this program, 22,511 people had participated, posing questions as large as whether to break up or propose marriage and as trivial as whether to dye their hair or grow a beard. Levitt then asked them to fill out a series of questionnaires, disclosing whether they followed the "advice" of the coin toss and estimating their happiness, both two months and six months later.

When push came to shove, not everyone was willing to let random chance dictate their life choices. But fully 63 percent of participants followed the coin toss, including more than half who faced major life changes.

Many of the results match what our usual intuition might tell us about such decisions. People who asked whether to "splurge" on some discretionary spending were less happy two months later if the coin said they should, but showed

---

* It was not a literal coin toss. A computer chose randomly between heads and tails.

no discernable difference after six months, suggesting some short-lived buyer's remorse but no long-term ill effects of small spending sprees. People who went on a diet as a result of the experiment tended to have the opposite experience, feeling happy after two months but neutral after six.*

But the most common question posed to Levitt's online coin flipper was a big one: Should I quit my job?

If you've read this far, you know that quitting your job will never solve all your problems. But that doesn't mean it's never the right decision, either. And in Levitt's experiment, quitting a job had *by far* the largest positive outcome on people's reported happiness after six months. They rated themselves on average *5 points higher* on a happiness scale of 1 to 10. That's like going from a miserable 3 to an ecstatic 8.

What does this tell us? As Levitt puts it, these results suggest that we tend to have "a substantial bias against making changes when it comes to important life decisions."[2] Specifically, we are biased against making big changes, when, in fact, "Those who do make a change report being no worse off after two months and much better off six months later." He concludes that, "Admonitions such as 'Winners never quit and quitters never win,' while well-meaning, may actually be extremely poor advice."

In a nutshell, sometimes quitters win.

---

* Presumably because the effects of most "diets" are short-lived. See *Buddha's Diet* to learn more about why.

To be clear, changing jobs is not always the right decision. Other research suggests that job satisfaction increases immediately after a job change, but then declines again over time.[3] And in many cases, the roots of our unhappiness are deeper than our work.

As with any big decision, the most important thing is to be clear about your motivations. Decisions that spring from those "unwholesome roots" of greed, hate, or delusion[4] are unlikely to be good ones.

So what are some good reasons to change jobs? Buddha felt that certain jobs were best avoided because they seemed intrinsically tied to suffering. These included dealing in weapons, human beings, meat, intoxicants, and poisons.[5] We might extend that to any job that directly harms others or damages the planet. He also discouraged his followers from all forms of fortune-telling or any other profession based on deceit.[6] Of course, it's up to you how to interpret these guidelines. In Buddha's time, he recommended against acting, because it seems he felt it was a form of deception.[7] These days, the entertainment industry is well established and well understood, so it seems strange to consider acting a form of lying. On the other hand, some might argue that Hollywood does propagate unhealthy and perhaps dishonest visions of the world—so perhaps it could be viewed as a form of lying after all.

Most jobs these days seem to fall into more of a gray area—good for the world in some ways, but perhaps bad for the world in others. My work in high tech is certainly no exception—helping people connect and communicate online lets them spread positive messages, but also negative ones. Publishing a book can be helpful to readers, yet consumes precious environmental resources. Even when I taught English to desperate refugees in Southeast Asia, some people felt our presence there encouraged vulnerable families to risk fleeing their country when it might have been wiser to stay. Judging any of my jobs or yours as good or bad may never be wholly clear-cut. You'll have to come to your own conclusions.

Many of us these days take a long time to find the right career. I had a series of unrelated jobs before starting in the tech industry, and spent over a decade in software engineering before discovering data science. I didn't publish my first book until well into my 40s. It's okay to try a few different things in the course of a lifetime, and to be honest with yourself about when you might have made the wrong choice—or when the right choice for some time in the past is not the right choice for you any longer.

Sometimes we're not the best judges of our own talents. Talk to people who know you well and know your work. Try to get an honest assessment of your strengths and weaknesses. Buddha didn't think at first that he'd be a good teacher. He was wrong! I once thought I could work as a male model in Japan.* I was wrong, too! Sometimes others see us more clearly than we see ourselves.

* True story.

It's not just about choosing a profession. Within any given field lies a wide range of companies, jobs, and bosses. Even the most humanitarian organization can have a tyrant in its midst, making all their employees miserable. Great careers may still have dead ends. The best reason to change jobs is to reduce suffering—including your own.

Of course, as we discussed in the previous chapter, not all job changes are voluntary. Try also to keep Buddha's guidance in mind if you are ever laid off or fired. Buddha saw no shame in unemployment and was a fierce defender of the morality of *not* working. Losing a job can be painful and frightening, and can bring real hardship. But it has no bearing on our intrinsic worth.

One of Buddha's central teachings was that nothing lasts forever. Our jobs, our careers—these are no exception. No matter what you do for a living, most of you will not die doing your current job. That means that, at some point, it will be time to walk away. According to the Bureau of Labor Statistics, the average American at age 50 has held about a dozen jobs since the age of 18—with half of those job changes occurring between 18 and 24![8]

For almost all of us, job change—even career change—is a fact of life. And that's good! It's good to fit many experiences into one lifetime. As Buddha put it: "Just as from a heap of flowers, many garlands can be made, so, you, with your mortal life, should do many skillful things."[9] Levitt's research suggests that we are collectively a bit too risk-averse about these transitions. In other words, the right time for a change may well be sooner than you think.

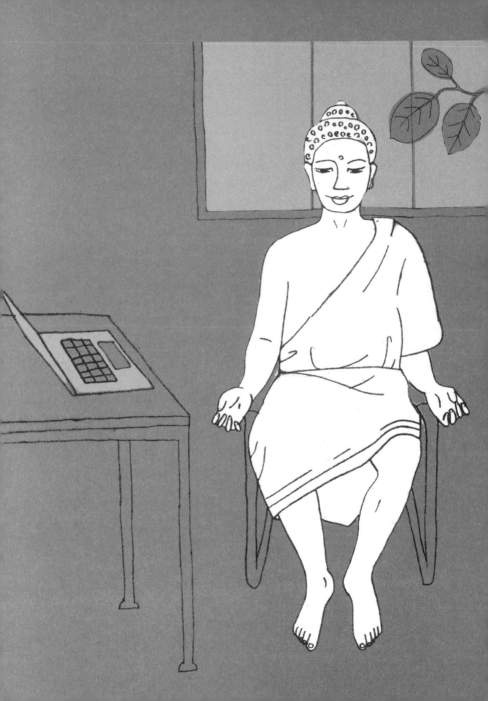

PART 4:

PERFECTIONS

CHAPTER 23

Data-Driven Dharma

BUDDHA DIDN'T DISCOVER MEDITATION AND MINDFULNESS and the rest of his path on day one. He spent six years trying other practices, studying with other teachers. To be honest, some of these sound a little nuts. He tried holding his breath for so long that his ears exploded, and even the gods assumed he was dead.[1] (Thankfully, he wasn't.) He tried extreme fasting, reducing down his daily meals until he was living on just a few drops of soup each day. He got so thin his arms looked like withered branches and the skin of his belly rested on his spine.[2]

Buddha was trying to do the same thing we're all trying to do. He wanted to stop suffering. He wanted to be happy. And he was willing to try *anything* to make that happen. He would travel any distance and learn from any teacher. Nothing was too far-fetched to be a worth a try.

In the end, Buddha didn't reject these crazy extremes of fasting and suffocating and the like because they were too hard. He abandoned them because they didn't work.

Buddha believed in data. Every time he tried something new, he paid attention. He collected evidence. He figured out what worked for him and what didn't. If something didn't work, he moved on. No moping or complaining. Buddha followed the data.

When Buddha finally had his awakening—when he actually became the Buddha—he insisted that all of us hold his teachings to the same standard. He didn't want any student to take his word on faith. He wanted us to test his teachings ourselves and to learn from our own experiences. "Do not go by oral tradition, by lineage of teaching, by hearsay, [or] by a collection of scripture," he admonished a student in one lecture.[3] In another passage he explained, "Something may be fully accepted out of faith, yet may be empty, hollow, and false; but something else may not be fully accepted out of faith, yet may be factual, true, and unmistaken."[4]

In other words, believing doesn't make it true.

You should apply this same skepticism to everything in this book. I've included numerous studies and stories here so you can learn from the data others have collected. But collect your own, too! See what works for you. See what doesn't. Experiment on your own life, just as Buddha experimented on his. Learn from your successes and your mistakes.

And keep asking hard questions when you get to work. One of my favorite things to ask when I'm listening to a presentation at the office is, "Why do you believe that?" I'm asking this not to be argumentative—although people sometimes take it that way!—but out of true curiosity. Sometimes there turns out to be good evidence for whatever the presenter is claiming. But oftentimes not. Often they have accepted that premise on faith, and are implicitly asking me to do the same. This can lead to a dangerous groupthink, where none of us realizes that our strategy is based on an unproven assumption.

On the other hand, the opposite situation also happens more often than you might think. People don't always realize how much they already know. Coworkers will want to go off and study a question that I'm pretty sure we can already answer—or at least answer well enough. People often search for certainty about things that are inherently uncertain, and misjudge when we know enough to move on.

As a simple illustration, imagine that you were asked the approximate population of the United States.* Maybe you remember reading this figure somewhere, but, if not, your first response might well be, "I have no idea." You'd tell them to go look it up.

But if you pause for a moment, you probably don't have *no* idea. Maybe you vaguely recall that China has around a billion people (it's actually a bit more). You're pretty sure the United States has fewer people than China, so now you know that the US population is under a billion. That's something!

Maybe, like me, you live in California, and you're pretty sure California has about 40 million people (it's actually a bit

---

* And let's assume you were asked this in the middle of the Utah desert, with no access to Google or Wikipedia or any other obvious source.

less). Of course, the whole United States encompasses more than just California, so now you know that the US population is more than 40 million. That's something, too!

Can we narrow things down a bit further? We just said that the United States encompasses more than just California—but how much more? Does half the United States live in California? That can't be right! Could it be a quarter? If California was a quarter of the United States, that means you could divide all 49 other states (plus Washington, DC) into just three groups, and each would be no bigger than California. That doesn't seem right, either. There are only two or three really big urban areas within California, and many more in all those other states. Could California comprise 10 percent of the US population then? That would mean you could divide the other states into nine groups the size of California—and that seems a bit more probable. There are probably a couple of California-sized clusters in the Northeast, maybe another in the Southeast, one around Texas, a few in the Midwest, one in the Northwest. I could see maybe coming up with about nine.

If California is about 10 percent of the United States, then the total population would be around 400 million. That turns out to be not a terrible estimate! (The actual number is around 327 million.) And it might be a good enough answer to satisfy the needs of whoever asked you.

In this example, we started out believing that we knew nothing. But we did know a little: We knew the rough population of China and California, and we knew a little about the relative size of the United States in comparison to those places. That may not sound like much, but it turned out to be enough.

When someone poses a tough question to me, I often ask myself what's the best answer I can give right now. Sometimes I really can't answer at all. But other times, on reflection, I realize that I know *something* that might be helpful. As long as I'm open about the limitations of this initial answer, there's no harm in sharing it. After all, a very rough estimate may be all they need.

Buddha asked us to follow the data. We can't do this unless we know what data we already have.

You can think of this as the flip side of beginner's mind. In beginner's mind, we accept and even embrace what we don't know. But we also need to be clear about what we *do* know. We must avoid the arrogance of assuming that we know everything, and also the arrogance of insisting that we know nothing. If you find yourself believing either of those extremes, you are probably wrong. Reality is almost always in between.

It's as important to be honest with yourself as with the people around you. Ask yourself hard questions—about your life *and* your work. Test your answers against the evidence. Pay attention to the data around you and learn from everything you try. Don't let willful arrogance or blind faith lead you astray.

CHAPTER 24

Living in the Present Moment

THERE'S A RISK TO ALL OUR TALK OF EFFORT AND GOALS, experiments and data. We might forget how amazing it is just to be alive.

Pause for a moment to consider the miracle of merely being here, now, and perhaps reading this book. So many things could have prevented this from happening. Life itself requires an incredibly complex and unlikely set of circumstances to exist. There are countless ways your own life could have ended before now. No matter how old you are today, many have died before your age. The fact that you are here, right now, is an amazing feat. But it's easy to lose sight of that when you're having a tough day.

Some work is boring. The most exciting job you can imagine generally involves at least occasional drudgery. We all have mundane or even unpleasant tasks that have to be completed. I sometimes find myself in meetings I wish I could skip, or filling out reports that I doubt anyone really needs. I have days when the California sun calls me to take a hike or a swim, and I'm stuck indoors dealing with some minor crisis.

Yet there is no such thing as mindless work—or at least

no such thing as work that needs to be mindless. The most basic, rote tasks lend themselves well to meditation. Zen monks in Japan are famous for doing seemingly mindless things like raking sand around the temple gardens of Kyoto, yet doing so with full presence and attention.

When I'm struggling to pay attention in a meeting, there's a temptation to start daydreaming about the things I'd rather do, counting the minutes until I can be somewhere else. (That's what I did in high school French class.) But instead of doing that, I try to do the opposite. I try to focus on exactly where I am. Sometimes I look around the room and try to see each individual as they truly are. I try to notice the expression on everyone's face—who is tense, who is happy, who is annoyed. I try to notice the color of their eyes. I'm often struck by how beautiful people are—ordinary people—when I really look at them. Each is a complete human being, with a life as rich and varied as my own. Each struggles with the same basic questions as I do—the same questions as Buddha did. Each wants to be happy.

When I start paying attention to the people in the meeting, I can't help paying attention to the meeting itself.

All of us have bad days. All of us get mad at our boss sometimes, or our coworkers or customers. All of us have moments when we wish we were somewhere else. But rather than taking that as our cue to disappear into mental fantasies, try to find something good about that exact moment. It doesn't have to be big. Maybe you hate your new assignment, but you love your chair. Maybe you love the outfit you chose that morning. Maybe you love the sound of the keys of your keyboard or the voice of a friendly officemate. If you can find something to love in *this* moment, then you can find something to love in the next moment, too. Because that's all life is—one moment after the other.

Wherever you are right now, try this experiment: Close your eyes (after you finish reading this paragraph), and listen to every single sound you can hear. Try not to judge them or to classify them or even to identify them—just hear them. If you can set aside your discriminating mind, there's as much music to the sound of rushing traffic as there is to a babbling brook. As I write this now, I can hear the steady hum of the refrigerator, the soft roar of water boiling in a tea kettle, the faint ticking of my watch, and a wayward bird or two chirping outside. Each of these has its own subtle beauty.

Try finding these glimpses of beauty in every moment. Much of working life seems to conspire against it. We're constantly pulled from one task to the next, forever thinking about everything else we have to do. The Vietnamese Zen master Thich Nhat Hanh explains that "We often become so busy that we forget what we are doing and even who we are."[1] Yet we can resist that slide into mindlessness and distraction. All we have to do is take this moment to be exactly where we are. As Thich Nhat Hanh goes on to say, "When we settle into the present moment, we can see beauties and wonders right before our eyes."[2]

Many of us experience that forgetting at work more than anywhere else. We think of work as what we do when we don't have a choice. But in every moment, we do have a choice. Even in the midst of the dullest or most annoying task, we can choose to be present, to pay attention. Whether it is raking sand or filling out spreadsheets or restocking the kitchen or folding sweaters, we can pause to appreciate the miracle of being here right now.

CHAPTER 25

Serving All Sentient Beings

AS BUDDHISM CONTINUED TO SPREAD AND EVOLVE throughout Asia, a new strand emerged and flourished that called itself the *Mahayana*, or "great vehicle." These teachers believed that our task here on earth is not just to realize our own awakening but to help others realize their awakening, too. They vowed not to depart this world for nirvana until everyone else could join them. And thus, according to the Mahayana tradition, we each only have one real job, which is called the bodhisattva vow—to save all beings from suffering.

Sounds easy, right?

OK, obviously, it's not easy. But it might not be as hard as you think.

There are many ways to help others. You don't have to become a doctor or a nurse. You don't have to travel to some war-ravaged land. You don't have to live among the poorest of the poor or the sickest of the sick. There's nothing wrong with any of those choices, of course, and some of you may feel called to do that.

But suffering is not just about pain or deprivation. It's not even *mostly* about pain or deprivation. Our material wealth and comfort have increased astronomically since Buddha's time, and yet the problem of suffering has persisted. The roots of suffering go deeper than the physical, so the bodhisattva vow extends well beyond offering material comfort and support.

Buddha himself didn't dedicate his life to feeding the poor. On the contrary, he expected the poor to feed him. He went out begging for alms every morning, even in the humblest villages, and ate only what the locals would give him. You see this same ritual in Buddhist countries today. The monks and nuns collect food from those around them—not, generally speaking, the other way around.*

Buddha didn't do this out of some sense of entitlement. He simply felt the greatest service he could offer was his own teaching. When the earliest Buddhist scriptures talk about "compassion," it is not about what we usually think of as helping each other out—it's entirely in the context of helping our fellow beings find awakening and end their own suffering. Buddha made this his life's work.

Again, this is not to say there's anything wrong with volunteering at your local soup kitchen or donating to charity. There isn't. Those are great things to do.

But you can help to end suffering without doing anything that looks or feels like charity. Practicing kindness to everyone you meet. Offering a smile or a hug to someone who's

---

* There are exceptions. The American Buddhist teacher Larry Yang tells the story of donating his extra alms to migrant laborers when he was a monk in Thailand.[1]

struggling. Speaking truth to those who need to hear it. Embodying calm in the face of chaos.

Most jobs provide countless opportunities like these for fulfilling our bodhisattva vow. Some are big, dramatic events, like responding with sympathy to a colleague with cancer or a dangerously ill child. But they can be smaller moments, too. The important thing is to take these chances when they come. I still remember the morning I interviewed for my last job. In the midst of a very stressful day, the receptionist greeted me with such warmth and kindness that she immediately put me at ease. I still thank her for this regularly, three years later.

When we see other people suffering, we're tempted to turn away. It's painful. Seeing their suffering makes us suffer. But facing that suffering is the heart of the bodhisattva vow. Everyone you work with is a human being. All of them are suffering. All of them wish they weren't. You can help.

Buddha didn't start out wanting to become a teacher. That wasn't why he left his palace home in the first place. His quest was to find answers for himself to life's great questions. Once he found his answers, he was content to float out into nirvana on his own. He didn't ask to be anyone's hero or savior. What got him teaching, and kept him engaged with the world, was his sense of compassion. He felt an obligation to help others find their own release from suffering, and for him teaching seemed like the best way.

You can find that same sense of purpose in your work. Everyone you meet at work presents an opportunity to practice compassion, to put others before yourself. Putting others first doesn't mean being a doormat. You shouldn't let your colleagues walk all over you. But you should treat each of them with respect—and even love. As we talked about before, even the most difficult messages can be delivered with kindness. As the Dalai Lama himself has said: "The main theme of Buddhism is altruism based on compassion and love."[2] The working world may seem like a strange place to practice such altruism, but it's not.

Don't stop there, either. You get plenty of opportunities to help others outside of work, too. A friend of mine befriended a homeless woman years ago and still puts her up in a local motel now and then when things are tough. Another friend paid for an immigration lawyer for her hairdresser. My older daughter is constantly finding lost pets and returning them to their owners. My younger daughter used to bring an extra lunch to school for a friend who seemed hungry. I've never worked as a lifeguard—I'm not nearly a strong enough swimmer—but I once fished a toddler from a swimming pool because I was in the right place at the right time and was paying attention.[3] Sometimes that's enough. No matter what you do for a living, you have the chance to be an amateur bodhisattva in your spare time if you pay attention, too.

Perhaps no one thought more about this practice than

Santideva, the early Mahayana monk in India, who wrote a whole book on the subject. The title of his masterwork is usually translated, quite appropriately, as "A Guide to the Bodhisattva Way of Life."[4] In it, he summarized the path this way: "One should do nothing other than what is either directly or indirectly of benefit to living beings."[5]

Bring that mission with you to your job, no matter what kind of work you do. Commit to using each interaction as a chance to make the world a little better. By paying attention to how everything you do affects those around you, you'll not only help them—you'll help yourself wake up, too.

CHAPTER 26

Did You Just Become a Buddhist?

THE UNITED STATES IS IN MANY RESPECTS AN UNUSUALLY religious country. Many Americans feel deep ties to their religious traditions—mostly as Christians, but with large and dedicated minorities of Jews, Muslims, Hindus, Buddhists, and others.

So let's say you've read this book and agree with everything I've written. (Thanks!) Did you just become a Buddhist?

You might think that anyone who agrees with Buddha's basic message—in other words, anyone who believes that Buddhism is true—would have to qualify as a Buddhist. And yet the author and philosopher Robert Wright *who actually wrote a book with that title*[1] doesn't call himself a Buddhist.

What gives? Wright explains his reasoning this way:

> I don't call myself a Buddhist, because traditional Buddhism has so many dimensions—of belief, of ritual—that I haven't adopted. I don't believe in reincarnation or related notions of karma, and I don't bow

before the statue of the Buddha upon entering the meditation hall, much less pray to him or any Buddhist deities. Calling myself a Buddhist, it seems to me, would almost be disrespectful to the many Buddhists, in Asia and elsewhere, who inherited and sustain a rich and beautiful religious tradition.[2]

I myself have taken a different approach. I *do* call myself a Buddhist, and have for most of my life. I even got ordained. Once in a while, I put on my traditional Buddhist robes and perform the same rituals that monks have carried out in Zen Buddhist temples across Japan for a thousand years, and which now occur all over the world. I don't believe in literal reincarnation or pray to Buddhist deities, but I do bow to statues of the Buddha when I see them, out of respect for the original teacher and his teachings.

But enough about me and some philosopher you've never met. What about you? Did *you* just become a Buddhist?

Of course, I can't possibly answer that question for you. Some people find sustenance and support in the long tradition of Buddhist practice that has brought forth the ideas discussed in this book. For them, identifying with that tradition and placing themselves in that lineage is comforting and perhaps helpful in developing a mindfulness practice. After all, while similar thoughts have occurred to those of other faiths, this particular rendering of mindfulness and related ideas derives from the specific line of teachers that began with Buddha about 2,500 years ago. When those two businessmen became the very first Buddhists, all they did was find refuge in the Buddha and his teachings. Perhaps you feel that you have found refuge, solace, or inspiration in them, too.

Others will still feel a strong tie to the religion of their birth. Perhaps despite appreciating Buddha's teachings, you still deeply believe in the teachings of Christ or Muhammad or another great religious figure outside of Buddhism. Perhaps you regularly attend a church or temple, synagogue or mosque. Perhaps you continue to pray at home.

There's nothing wrong with any of those choices. There is a story in the sutras of a wealthy householder named Upali who meets Buddha and becomes his disciple. He is so enamored of his newfound faith that he tells the Buddha that, from then on, he will make donations only to Buddha and his followers and not to his previous spiritual teachers. (They were apparently Jains, another ancient Indian religion.) Buddha says no, that Upali's family has long supported these other teachers and that he should continue to do so.[3] Buddha is happy to accept Upali as a student, but he sees no reason for him to cut himself off from his past.

Buddhism is not a faith that asks you to be exclusive or to give up any other beliefs. Buddhism doesn't really ask you to believe *anything* exactly. As I hope you've discovered already, Buddhism is much more about *doing* things, *practicing* things, having experiences rather than beliefs, and then paying attention to those experiences and the results. You can put Buddhist labels on those practices and experiences. You can call yourself a Buddhist and talk about enlightenment and awakening in Buddhist terms. Or not.

This book was not intended to make you a Buddhist. My goal was much more modest—and much grander at the same time. My goal was to help you use some of Buddha's teachings to be happier and to suffer less—primarily at work, but also anywhere else you happen to spend time. And not just fleetingly happy, but truly, deeply happy—what Buddhists would call awakened, which turns out to be the same thing.

Most of the techniques we've discussed probably don't even feel very religious or spiritual to you. Pay attention. Look for balance. Eat well, sleep well, and exercise regularly. Set healthy goals. Work hard, but not too long. Tell the truth. Be kind.

Buddha didn't care if you became a Buddhist, either, by the way. He just wanted you to become a Buddha. I think you can.

Now get to work.

CHAPTER 27

Further Reading

IF YOU WANT TO LEARN MORE ABOUT BUDDHISM, I HAVE good news and bad news. The good news is that there are *lots* of books about Buddhism. The bad news is that there are *lots* of books about Buddhism.

The Buddhist scriptures themselves are often challenging for modern readers, but Martine Batchelor's *The Spirit of the Buddha* (New Haven, CT: Yale University Press, 2010) includes many selections in a clear and approachable style and is a wonderful introduction, as is Gil Fronsdal's *The Dhammapada* (Boston: Shambhala Publications, 2006), a lyrical translation of Buddha's best-known sayings. If you insist on going straight to the unabridged originals, the editions I cite in my "Notes on Sources" are my favorite translations.

Most readers will find the writings of contemporary Buddhist teachers much more accessible. I particularly like Stephen Batchelor's* *Buddhism Without Beliefs* (New York: Riverhead Books, 1997) and Robert Wright's *Why Buddhism Is True* (New York: Simon & Schuster, 2017), both of which

---

* Yes, he's Martine's husband. The Batchelors may be the first Buddhist power couple in the West.

attempt to strip away the more "mystical" aspects of Buddha's teachings and focus on practical practice. For a more "Buddhist" introduction to Buddhism, Thubten Chodron's *Buddhism for Beginners* (Boston: Snow Lion, 2001) is excellent, as is Zenju Earthlyn Manuel's priceless gem *Tell Me Something About Buddhism* (Charlottesville: Hampton Roads, 2011).

To learn more about the nuts and bolts of meditation, Shunryu Suzuki's *Zen Mind, Beginner's Mind* (Boston: Shambhala Publications, 2004) is the classic introduction to the Zen way (which I practice), while Kathleen McDonald's *How to Meditate* (Somerville, MA: Wisdom Publications, 2005) approaches the topic from the Tibetan tradition. If you want to know more about Buddha himself, John S. Strong's *The Buddha: A Beginner's Guide* (Oxford, UK: Oneworld Publications, 2001) is surprisingly great, as is Karen Armstrong's popular *Buddha* (New York: Penguin, 2004).

On the work front, Mike Steib's *Career Manifesto* (New York: TarcherPerigee, 2018) will walk you through how to establish healthy career goals. Alex Soojun-Kim Pang's wonderful *The Distraction Addiction* (New York: Little, Brown and Company, 2013) discusses the crucial issue of distraction and technology in far more detail than I have here and is well worth reading. Kim Scott's eye-opening *Radical Candor* (New York: St. Martin's Press, 2017) will teach you, as she puts it, "to be a kick-ass boss without losing your humanity," and is essential reading for anyone who aspires to be an honest manager.

Joseph Emet has written a whole book on mindful techniques for better sleep: *Buddha's Book of Sleep: Sleep Better in Seven Weeks with Mindfulness Meditation* (New York: TarcherPerigee, 2012). If you've chosen yoga as your preferred exercise—an excellent choice!—Eddie Stern's *One Simple Thing* (New York: North Point Press, 2019) will be an invaluable companion.

My first book, *Buddha's Diet*, cowritten with my dear friend Tara Cottrell, has lots more to say about diet and exercise (and Buddhism, too). These are incredibly important topics that we've only touched on here. Getting that part of your life in order will really pay off at work. If you liked this book, you'll probably like *Buddha's Diet*. And if you didn't like this book, you shouldn't be asking me for reading advice.

Acknowledgments

THIS BOOK WOULDN'T HAVE BEEN POSSIBLE WITHOUT my family, who indulged all my writing time over the last year when perhaps I should have been more focused on them. Thank you, Dina, Anna, and Maxine. My agent, Laura Dail, and editor, Jennifer Kasius, believed in this book long before I did, and provided much-needed encouragement and patience while I wrote it. Although I couldn't convince her to write this one with me, my writing partner and friend Tara Cottrell continues to be an inspiration and support, and texted me many good ideas as I wrote. My friend Irina Reyn offered critical perspective when I was struggling to make progress and helped me see what this book could become.

I've worked at many companies over the years and learned from all of them. Those jobs gave me space to think more deeply about the connection between my Buddhist practice and my working life, which then formed the basis for much of what I've written here.

I started writing this book in earnest during a brief stay at Tassajara Zen Mountain Center. I am grateful to everyone who welcomed me there and who helps maintain that unique Buddhist presence in the West.

Notes on Sources

THE PALI TEXT SOCIETY, A VENERABLE BRITISH INSTITU-
tion founded by intrepid scholars in 1881 and still going
strong, established a comprehensive system for citing the
ancient Buddhist scriptures so that the same passage can be
found in any translation, in much the same way that one can
look up "Luke 6:31" in any edition of the New Testament.
Alas, the Buddhist system is very complicated (a typical reference looks like this: "SN 22.59; III 67, 25"), and I have
not used it here. Instead, I give simple page references using
my favorite translations of each text, which is usually Wisdom Publications' beautiful *Teachings of the Buddha* series.
This will be much simpler for most readers, although more
challenging if you want to find the equivalent passage in
some other translation. I follow this same practice for non-
Pali scriptures, simply citing the specific translation that I
prefer to use.

Endnotes

INTRODUCTION: WAKING UP AT WORK

1 U.S. Travel Association, Project: Time Off, *The State of the American Vacation* (2018).

2 Joel Goh, Jeffrey Pfeffer, and Stefanos A. Zenios, "The Relationship between Workplace Stressors and Mortality and Health Costs in the United States," *Management Science* (2016) 62:2: 608–628. https://doi.org/10.1287/mnsc.2014.2115.

3 Caroline Foley Rhys Davids. "Notes on Early Economic Conditions in Northern India," *Journal of the Royal Asiatic Society of Great Britain and Ireland* (1901): 859–888. http://www.jstor.org/stable/25208356.

CHAPTER 1: WHY WORK?

1 I. B. Horner, *The Book of Discipline*, vol. IV (Oxford, UK: The Pali Text Society, 1951), 5–6.

2 Mohan Wijyayaranta, *Buddhist Monastic Life: According to the Sources of the Theravada Tradition* (Cambridge, UK: Cambridge University Press, 1990), 164.

3 Bhikkhu Bodhi, *The Numerical Discourses of the Buddha* (Somerville, MA: Wisdom Publications, 2012), 112.

4 Rupert Gethin, *Sayings of the Buddha* (Oxford, UK: Oxford University Press, 2008), 10.

5 Mike Steib expands on this in his wonderful *Career Manifesto: Discover Your Calling and Create an Extraordinary Life* (New York: TarcherPedigree, 2018), although he revised it to "learn, earn, serve," which I find less catchy.

6 Bhikkhu Bodhi, *The Suttanipata* (Somerville, MA: Wisdom Publications, 2017), 223 and 863.

7 Ibid., 291.

8 Bhikkhu Bodhi, *The Connected Discourses of the Buddha* (Somerville, MA: Wisdom Publications, 2000), 1597.

9 Bodhi, *The Suttanipata*, 199.

CHAPTER 2: THE COST OF SUFFERING

1 See, for example, Thanissaro Bhikkhu, *The Wings to Awakening: An Anthology from the Pali Canon* (Valley Center, CA: Metta Forest Monastery, 2018).

2 National Institute for Occupational Safety and Health, "STRESS…at Work," Centers for Disease Control and Prevention. https://www.cdc.gov/niosh/docs/99-101/.

3 Madhu Kalia, "Assessing the Economic Impact of Stress—The Modern Day Hidden Epidemic," *Metabolism* 51, no. 6, supplement 1 (June 2002): 49–53.

4 Joanne H. Gavin and Richard O. Mason, "The Virtuous

Organization: The Value of Happiness in the Workplace," *Organizational Dynamics* 33, no. 4 (2014): 379–392

5 D. M. Rose, A. Seidler, M. Nübling, U. Latza, E. Brähler, E. M. Klein, J. Wiltink, M. Michal, S. Nickels, P. S. Wild, J. König, M. Claus, S. Letzel and M. E. Beutel, "Associations of Fatigue to Work-Related Stress, Mental and Physical Health in an Employed Community Sample," *BMC Psychiatry* 17, no. 1 (May 5, 2017):167. doi: 10.1186/s12888-017-1237-y.

6 Kristina Holmgren, Synneve Dahlin-Ivanoff, Cecilia Björkelund, and Gunnel Hensing, "The Prevalence of Work-Related Stress, and Its Association with Self-Perceived Health and Sick-Leave, in a Population of Employed Swedish Women," *BMC Public Health* 9 (2009): 73. doi: 10.1186/1471-2458-9-73.

7 Daniel C. Ganster and John Schaubroeck, "Work Stress and Employee Health," *Journal of Management* 17, issue 2 (June 1, 1991): 235–227. doi: 10.1177/014920639101700202.

8 Kalia, "Assessing the Economic Impact of Stress."

9 Helge Hoel, "The Cost of Violence/Stress at Work and the Benefits of a Violence/Stress-Free Working Environment," Report Commissioned by the International Labour Organization (2001). http://www.ilo.org/safework/info/publications/WCMS_108532/lang—en/index.htm

10 Jeffrey Pfeffer, *Dying for a Paycheck* (New York: Harper Collins, 2018), 1.

11 Kalia, "Assessing the Economic Impact of Stress."

12 T. A. Wright and B. A. Straw, "Affect and Favorable Work Outcomes: Two Longitudinal Tests of the Happy-Productive Worker Thesis," *Journal of Organizational Behavior* 20 (1999): 1–23.

13 Andrew J. Oswald, Eugenio Proto, and Daniel Sgroi, "Happiness and Productivity," *Journal of Labor Economics* 33, no. 4 (2015): 789–822.

14 Cynthia D. Fisher, "Happiness at Work," *International Journal of Management Reviews* 12 (2010): 384–412. doi:10.1111/j.1468-2370.2009.00270.x.

15 John M. Zelenski, Steven A. Murphy, and David A. Jenkins, "The Happy-Productive Worker Thesis Revisited," *Journal of Happiness Studies* 9, issue 4 (December 2008): 521–537. doi: 10.1007/s10902-008-9087-4.

16 Lisa C. Walsh, "Does Happiness Promote Career Success? Revisiting the Evidence," *Journal of Career Assessment* 26, issue 2 (2018): 199–219.

CHAPTER 3: BUDDHISM WAS A START-UP

1 Heinz Bechert, *When Did the Buddha Live?: Controversy on the Dating of the Historical Buddha* (New Delhi, India: Sri Satguru Publications, 1995).

2 Christopher Titmuss, *The Political Buddha* (Morrisville, NC, Lulu.com: 2018).

3 Bhikkhu Bodhi, *The Numerical Discourses of the Buddha* (Somerville, MA: Wisdom Publications, 2012), 240 and 1642.

4 Edward Conze, *Buddhist Scriptures* (London: Penguin Books, 1959), 39.

5 Bhikkhu Nanamoli and Bhikkhu Bodhi, *The Middle Length Discourses of the Buddha* (Somerville, MA: Wisdom Publications, 1995), 260.

6 Ibid., 534.

7 Moshe Walshe, *The Long Discourses of the Buddha* (Somerville, MA: Wisdom Publications, 1987), 408.

8 Bhikkhu Bodhi, *The Suttanipata* (Somerville, MA: Wisdom Publications, 2017), 178.

9 Walshe, *The Long Discourses of the Buddha*, 270.

10 Bhikkhu Bodhi, *The Connected Discourses of the Buddha* (Somerville, MA: Wisdom Publications, 2000), 1644.

CHAPTER 4: BUDDHA'S BIG IDEA

1 H. W. Schuman, *The Historical Buddha: The Times, Life and Teachings of the Founder of Buddhism*, translated by M. O'C Walshe (Delhi, India: Motilal Banarsidass Publishers, 1989), 22.

2 Mathew Meghaprasara, *New Guide to the Tipitaka: A Complete Reference to the Buddhist Canon* (Regina, Saskatchewan: A Sangha of Books, 2013), 5–6.

3 Schuman, *The Historical Buddha*, 4.

4 Richard Solomon, *The Buddhist Literature of Ancient Gandhāra* (Somerville, MA: Wisdom Publications, 2018), 1–3

5 See, for example: Cheri Huber, *Suffering is Optional* (Murphys, CA: Keep It Simple Books, 2000).

CHAPTER 5: PAYING ATTENTION

1 Jon Kabat-Zinn, "An Outpatient Program in Behavioral Medicine for Chronic Pain Patients Based on the Practice of Mindfulness Meditation: Theoretical Considerations and Preliminary Results," *General Hospital Psychiatry* 4, issue 1 (April 1982): 33–47.

2 Bhikkhu Nanamoli and Bhikkhu Bodhi, *The Middle Length Discourses of the Buddha* (Somerville, MA: Wisdom Publications, 1995), 145.

3 Nyanaponika Thera, *The Power of Mindfulness* (San Francisco: Unity Press, 1972), 5.

4 Kirk Warren Brown and Richard M. Ryan, "The Benefits of Being Present: Mindfulness and Its Role in Psychological Well-Being," *Journal of Personality and Social Psychology* 84, no. 4 (2003): 822–848.

5 Darren Good, Christopher J. Lyddy, Theresa M. Glomb, Joyce E. Bono, Kirk Warren Brown, Michelle K. Duffy, Ruth A. Baer, Judson A. Brewer, Sara W. Lazar, "Contemplating

Mindfulness at Work: An Integrative Review," *Journal of Management* (January 2016). doi: 10.1177/0149206315617003.

6 Maryanna Klatt, Beth Steinberg, and Anne-Marie Duchemin, "*Mindfulness in Motion* (MIM): An Onsite Mindfulness Based Intervention (MBI) for Chronically High Stress Work Environments to Increase Resiliency and Work Engagement," *Journal of Visualized Experiments* 101 (2015), e52359. doi:10.3791/52359.

7 Amishi P. Jha Elizabeth A. Stanley, Anastasia Kiyonaga, Ling Wong, and Lois Gelfand, "Examining the Protective Effects of Mindfulness Training on Working Memory Capacity and Affective Experience," *Emotion* 10, no. 1 (2010): 54–64.

8 Patrick K. Hyland, R. Andrew Lee and Maura J. Mills, "Mindfulness at Work: A New Approach to Improving Individual and Organizational Performance," *Industrial and Organizational Psychology* 8, no. 4 (December 2014): 576–602. doi: 10.1017/iop.2015.41.

9 Ruth Q. Wolever, Kyra J. Bobinet, Kelley McCabe, Elizabeth R. Mackenzie, Erin Fekete, Catherine A. Kusnick, Michael Baime, "Effective and Viable Mind-Body Stress Reduction in the Workplace: A Randomized Controlled Trial," *Journal of Occupational Health Psychology* 17, no. 2 (2012): 246–258. doi: 10.1037/a0027278.

10 Kimberly Schaufenbuel, "Why Google, Target, and General Mills Are Investing in Mindfulness," *Harvard Business Review* (December 28, 2015).

CHAPTER 6: MEDITATE LIKE A BUDDHA

1 Bhikkhu Nanamoli and Bhikkhu Bodhi, *The Middle Length Discourses of the Buddha* (Somerville, MA: Wisdom Publications, 1995), 260.

2 See, for example, Bhikkhu Analyao, *Satipatthana: The Direct Path to Realization* (Cambridge, UK: Windhorse Publications, 2003).

3 Nanamoli and Bodhi, *The Middle Length Discourses of the Buddha*, 145.

4 Ibid., 146.

5 Ibid., 155.

6 Ibid., 147.

7 Gil Frondsal, *The Dhammapada* (Boulder, CO: Shamabhala Publications, 2005), 1.

8 Peter W. Mayer and William B. DeOreo, "Residential Uses of Water," *American Water Works Association* (1999).

9 His Holiness the 14th Dalai Lama of Tibet, "Routine Day," DalaiLama.com. http://www.dalailama.com/the-dalai-lama/biography-and-daily-life/a-routine-day

CHAPTER 7: THE PROBLEM WITH EXPERTISE

1 Carl Bielfeld, *Dogen's Manual of Zen Meditation* (Berkeley: University of California Press, 1988), 195.

2 Eleanor Rosch, "Beginner's Mind: Paths to the Wisdom Not Learned," in *Teaching for Wisdom*, edited by Michal Merrari and Georges Potworowski (New York: Springer Science+Business Media, 2008).

3 Shunryu Suzuki, *Zen Mind, Beginner's Mind* (New York: Weatherhill, 1970), 21.

4 Ibid., 21.

5 Joe Langford and Pauline Rose Clance, "The Impostor Phenomenon: Recent Research Findings Regarding Dynamics, Personality and Family Patterns and Their Implications for Treatment," *Psychotherapy Theory Research & Practice* 30, no. 3 (December 1992): 495–501. doi: 10.1037/0033-3204.30.3.495.

6 Albert J. Stunkard, "Beginner's Mind: Trying to Learn Something About Obesity," *Annals of Behavioral Medicine* 13, issue 2, (January 1, 1991): 51–56. https://doi.org/10.1093/abm/13.2.51.

7 Arlo Belshee, "Promiscuous Pairing and Beginner's Mind: Embrace Inexperience," in *Proceedings of AGILE 2005* (Piscataway, NJ: IEEE, 2005). doi: 10.1109/ADC.2005.37

8 Sheryl I. Fontaine, "Teaching with the Beginner's Mind: Notes from My Karate Journal," *College Composition and Communication* 54, no. 2 (December 2002): 208–221. doi: 10.2307/1512146

9 Mark Stefik and Barbara Stefik, "The Prepared Mind versus the Beginner's Mind," *Design Management Review* 16, no. 1 (Winter 2005): 10–16.

10 Kate Crosby and Andrew Skilton, *The Bodhicaryavatra* (Oxford, UK: Oxford University Press, 1995), 40.

CHAPTER 8: WORKING WITHOUT WORKING

1 Robert A. Henning, Pierre Jacques, George V. Kissel, Anne B. Sullivan and Sabina M. Alteras-Webb, "Frequent Short Rest Breaks from Computer Work: Effects on Productivity and Well-Being at Two Field Sites," *Ergonomics* 40, no. 1 (1997): 78–91.

2 Simone M. Ritter and Ap Dijksterhuis, "Creativity—The Unconscious Foundations of the Incubation Period," *Frontiers in Human Neuroscience* 8 (2014): 215. doi: 10.3389/fnhum.2014.00215.

3 Charlotte Fritz, Allison M. Ellis, Caitlin A. Demsky, Bing C. Lin, and Frankie Guros, "Embracing work breaks: Recovering from Work Stress," *Organizational Dynamics* 42, (2013): 274–280.

4 Sooyeol Kim, Youngah Park, and Lucille Headrick, "Employees' Micro-Break Activities and Job Performance: An Examination of Telemarketing Employees," *Academy of Management Annual Meeting Proceedings* 1 (2015): 13,943–13,943. doi: 10.5465/AMBPP.2015.169.

5 Pavle Mijovic, Vanja Kovic, Ivan Mačužić, Petar Todorović, Branislav Jeremić, Miloš Milovanović, and Ivan Gligorijević, "Do Micro-Breaks Increase the Attention Level of an Assembly Worker? An ERP Study," *Procedia Manufacturing* 3 (2015): 5074–5080.

6   Brent L. S. Coker, "Freedom to Surf: The Positive Effects of Workplace Internet Leisure Browsing," *New Technology, Work and Employment* 26, issue 3 (2011): 238–247. doi: 10.1111/j.1468-005X.2011.00272.x

7   Fritz, et al., "Embracing Work Breaks."

8   Hongjai Rhee and Sudong Kim, "Effects of Breaks on Regaining Vitality at Work: An Empirical Comparison of 'Conventional' and 'Smart Phone' Breaks," *Computers in Human Behavior* 57 (2016): 160–167. doi: 10.1016/j.chb.2015.11.056.

9   Marianna Virtanen, Archana Singh-Manoux, Jane E. Ferrie, David Gimeno, Michael G. Marmot, Marko Elovainio, Markus Jokela, Jussi Vahtera, and Mika Kivimäki, "Long Working Hours and Cognitive Function: The Whitehall II Study," *American Journal of Epidemiology* 169, issue 5 (March 1, 2009): 596–605. https://doi.org/10.1093/aje/kwn382.

10 Erin Reid. "Embracing, Passing, Revealing, and the Ideal Worker Image: How People Navigate Expected and Experienced Professional Identities," *Organization Science* 26, no. 4 (2015): 997–1017. doi:10.1287/ORSC.2015.0975.

11 Thich Nhat Hanh, *Begin Peace* (Berkeley, CA: Parallax Press, 1987), 47.

12 Alex Soojung-Kim Pang, "How Resting More Can Boost Your Productivity," *Greater Good Magazine* (May 11, 2017).

CHAPTER 9: BUDDHA ON THE BUS

1 J. N. Morris, J. A. Heady, P. A. B. Raffle, C. G. Roberts, and J. W. Parks, "Coronary Heart Disease and Physical Activity of Work," *Lancet* 262, no. 6795 (1953): 1053–1057. https://doi.org/10.1016/S0140-6736(53)90665-5.

2 Laura E. Finch, A. Janet Tomiyama, and Andrew Ward, "Taking a Stand: The Effects of Standing Desks on Task Performance and Engagement," *International Journal of Environmental Research and Public Health* 14, no. 8 (August 2017): 939. doi: 10.3390/ijerph14080939.

3 Frank W. Booth, Christian K. Roberts, John P. Thyfault, Gregory N. Ruegsegger, and Ryan G. Toedebusch, "Role of Inactivity in Chronic Diseases: Evolutionary Insight and Pathophysiological Mechanisms," *Physiology Review* 97, no. 4 (October 1, 2017): 1351–1402. doi: 10.1152/physrev.00019.2016.

4 I-Min Lee, Eric J Shiroma, Felipe Lobelo, Pekka Puska, Steven N Blair, Pand Peter T .Katzmarzyk, "Impact of Physical Inactivity on the World's Major Non-Communicable Diseases," *Lancet* 380, no. 9838 (July 21, 2012): 219–229. doi: 10.1016/S0140-6736(12)61031-9.

5 Andreas Ströhle, "Physical activity, exercise, depression and anxiety disorders," *Journal of Neural Transmission* (Vienna) 116, no. 6 (June 2009): 777–784. doi: 10.1007/s00702-008-0092-x.

6   Helen E. Brown, Nicholas D. Gilson, Nicola W. Burton, and Wendy J. Brown. "Does Physical Activity Impact on Presenteeism and Other Indicators of Workplace Well-Being?," *Sports Medicine* 41 (2011): 249. https://doi.org/10.2165/11539180-000000000-00000

7   Candice L. Hogan, Jutta Mata, and Laura L. Carstensen, "Exercise Holds Immediate Benefits for Affect and Cognition in Younger and Older Adults," *Psychology and Aging* 28, no. 2 (June 2013: 587–594. doi:10.1037/a0032634.

8   Marily Oppezzo and Daniel L. Schwartz, "Give Your Ideas Some Legs: The Positive Effect of Walking on Creative Thinking," *Journal of Experimental Psychology: Learning, Memory, and Cognition* 40, no. 4 (2014): 1142–1152.

9   Nicolaas P. Pronk, Brian Martinson, Ronald Kessler, Arne Beck, Gregory Simon, and Philip Wang, "The Association between Work Performance and Physical Activity, Cardiorespiratory Fitness, and Obesity," *Journal of Occupational and Environmental Medicine* 46, no. 1 (January 2004): 19–25.

10 J. C. Coulson, J. McKenna, and M. Field, "Exercising at work and self-reported work performance," *International Journal of Workplace Health Management* 1, issue 3 (2008): 176–197. https://doi.org/10.1108/17538350810926534.

11 Emmanuel Stamatakis, Ngaire Coombs, Alex Rowlands, Nicola Shelton, and Melvyn Hillsdon, "Objectively-Assessed and Self-Reported Sedentary Time in Relation to Multiple

Socioeconomic Status Indicators among Adults in England: A Cross-Sectional Study," *BMJ Open* 4 (2014) e006034. doi:10.1136/ bmjopen-2014-006034.

12 Hidde P. van der Ploeg, Tien Chey, Rosemary J. Korda, Emily Banks, and Adrian Bauman, "Sitting Time and All-Cause Mortality Risk in 222,497 Australian Adults," *Archives of Internal Medicine* 172, no. 6 (2012): 494–500. doi:10.1001/ archinternmed.2011.2174.

13 Avner Ben-Ner, Darla J. Hamann, Gabriel Koepp, Chimnay U. Manohar, and James Levine, "Treadmill Workstations: The Effects of Walking While Working on Physical Activity and Work Performance," *PLOS ONE* 9, no. 2 (2014): e88620. https://doi.org/10.1371/journal.pone.0088620.

14 Avner Ben-Ner, Darla J. Hamann, Gabriel Koepp, and James Levine, "The Effects of Walking while Working on Productivity and Health: A Field Experiment" (May 2, 2012). Available at SRN: https://ssrn.com/abstract=2547437 or http://dx.doi.org/10.2139/ssrn.2547437.

15 Brittany T. MacEwen, Dany J. MacDonald, and Jamie F. Burr, "A Systematic Review of Standing and Treadmill Desks in the Workplace," *Preventive Medicine* 70 (2015): 50–58. doi: 10.1016/j.ypmed.2014.11.011.

16 Christi S. Ulmer, Barbara A. Stetson, and Paul G. Salmon, "Mindfulness and Acceptance Are Associated with Exercise Maintenance in YMCA Exercisers," *Behavioral Research and*

Therapy 48, no. 8 (August 2010): 805–809. doi: 10.1016/j. brat.2010.04.009.

17 Katy Tapper, Christine Shaw, Joanne Ilsley, Andrew J. Hill, Frank W. Bond, Laurence Moore, "Exploratory randomised controlled trial of a mindfulness-based weight loss intervention for women," *Appetite* 52, issue 2 (April 2009): 396–404. https://doi.org/10.1016/j.appet.2008.11.012.

18 Teresa D. Hawkes, Wayne Manselle, and Marjorie H. Woollacott, "Cross-Sectional Comparison of Executive Attention Function in Normally Aging Long-Term *T'ai Chi*, Meditation, and Aerobic Fitness Practitioners Versus Sedentary Adults," *Journal of Alternative and Complementary Medicine* 20, no. 3 (March 1, 2014): 178–184. doi: 10.1089/ acm.2013.0266.

19 Anu Kangasniemi, Raimo Lappalainen, AnnaKankaanpää, and TuijaTammelin, "Mindfulness Skills, Psychological Flexibility, and Psychological Symptoms among Physically Less Active and Active Adults," *Mental Health and Physical Activity* 7, issue 3 (2014): 121–127. https://doi.org/10.1016/j. mhpa.2014.06.005.

20 Fumio Shaku, Madoka Tsutsumi, Hideyoshi Goto, and Denise Saint Arnoult, "Measuring the Effects of Zen Training on Quality of Life and Mental Health among Japanese Monk Trainees: A Cross-Sectional Study," *Journal of Alternative and Complementary Medicine* 20, no. 5 (May 2014): 406–410. doi: 10.1089/acm.2013.0209.

21 Fabiana Braga Benatti and Mathias Ried-Larsen, "The Effects of Breaking up Prolonged Sitting Time: A Review of Experimental Studies," *Medicine & Science in Sports & Exercise* 47, no. 10 (October 2015): 2053–2061. doi: 10.1249/ MSS.0000000000000654.

22 Markus D. Jakobsen, Emil Sundstrup, Mikkel Brandt, and Lars L. Andersen, "Psychosocial Benefits of Workplace Physical Exercise: Cluster Randomized Controlled Trial," *BMC Public Health* 17 (2017): 798. doi: 10.1186/s12889-017-4728-3.

23 James H. O'Keefe, Carl J. Lavie, and Marco Guazzi, "Part 1: Potential Dangers of Extreme Endurance Exercise: How Much Is Too Much? Part 2: Screening of School-Age Athletes," *Progress in Cardiovascular Diseases* 57, issue 4 (2014). doi: 10.1016/j.pcad.2014.11.004.

24 Kate Crosby and Andrew Skilton, *The Bodhicaryavatra* (Oxford, UK: Oxford University Press, 1995), 103.

25 O'Keefe et al., "Part 1: Potential Dangers of Extreme Endurance Exercise: How Much Is Too Much? Part 2: Screening of School-Age Athletes."

26 Stéphane Brutus, Roshan Javadian, and Alexandra Joelle Panaccio, "Cycling, Car, or Public Transit: A Study of Stress and Mood upon Arrival at Work," *International Journal of Workplace Health Management* 10, no. 1 (2017) 13–24. https://doi.org/10.1108/IJWHM-10-2015-0059.

27 Crosby and Skilton, *The Bodhicaryavatra*, 26.

CHAPTER 10: SLEEPING TO WAKE UP

1 Moshe Walshe, *The Long Discourses of the Buddha* (Somerville, MA: Wisdom Publications, 1987), 463.

2 Gil Frondsal, *The Dhammapada* (Boulder, CO: Shamabhala Publications, 2005), 84.

3 Ariana Huffington, *The Sleep Revolution* (New York: Harmony Books, 2017), 3.

4 Michael A. Grandner, "Sleep, Health, and Society," *Journal of Clinical Sleep Medicine* 12, no. 1 (March 2017): 1–22. doi: 10.1016/j.jsmc.2016.10.012. Epub December 20, 2016.

5 E. R. Kucharczyk, K. Morgan, and A. P. Hall, "The Occupational Impact of Sleep Quality and Insomnia Symptoms," *Sleep Medicine Review* 16, no. 6 (December 2012): 547–559. doi: 10.1016/j.smrv.2012.01.005.

6 R.C. Kessler, Patricia A. Berglund, Catherine Coulouvrat, Goeran Hajak, Thomas Roth, Victoria Shahly, Alicia C. Shillington, Judith J. Stephenson, and James K. Walsh, "Insomnia and the Performance of US Workers: Results from the America Insomnia Survey," *Sleep* 34, no. 9 (September 1, 2011): 1161–1171. doi: 10.5665/SLEEP.1230.

7 Mark B. Rosekind, Kevin B. Gregory, Melissa M. Mallis, Summer L. Brandt, Brian Seal,and Debra Lerner, "The Cost of Poor Sleep: Workplace Productivity Loss and Associated Costs," *Journal of Occupational and Environmental Medicine* 52, no. 1 (January 2010): 91–98. doi: 10.1097/JOM.0b013e3181c78c30.

8 Matthew Gibson and Jeffrey Shrader, "Time Use and Productivity: The Wage Returns to Sleep," *Review of Economics and Statistics* 100, no. 5 (2018), 783–798. https://doi.org/10.1162/rest_a_00746.

9 Irshaad O. Ebrahim, Colin M. Shapiro, Adrian J. Williams, and Peter B. Fenwick, "Alcohol and Sleep I: Effects on Normal Sleep," *Alcoholism Clinical and Experimental Research.* 37, no. 4 (April 2013): 539–549. doi: 10.1111/acer.12006.

10 Michael Gradisar, Amy R. Wolfson, Allison G. Harvey, Lauren Hale, Russell Rosenberg, and Charles A. Czeisler, "The Sleep and Technology Use of Americans: Findings from the National Sleep Foundation's 2011 Sleep in America Poll," *Journal of Clinical Sleep Medicine* 9, no. 12 (December 15, 2013): 1291–1299. doi: 10.5664/jcsm.3272.

11 Anne-Marie Chang, Daniel Aeschbach, Jeanne F. Duffy, and Charles A. Czeislera, "Evening Use of Light-Emitting eReaders Negatively Affects Sleep, Circadian Timing, and Next-Morning Alertness," *Proceedings of the National Academy of Sciences* USA 112, no. 4 (January 2015): 1232–1237. doi: 10.1073/pnas.1418490112.

12 YongMin Cho, Seung-Hun Ryu, Byeo Ri Lee, Kyung Hee Kim, Eunil Lee, and Jaewook Choi, "Effects of artificial light at night on human health: A literature review of observational and experimental studies applied to exposure assessment," *Chronobiology International* 32, no. 9 (2015): 1294–1310. doi: 10.3109/07420528.2015.1073158.

13 Jitendra M. Mishra, "A Case for Naps in the Workplace," *Seidman Business Review* 15, issue 1, Article 9 (2009).

14 Mark R. Rosekind Roy M. Smith, Donna L. Miller, Elizabeth L. Co, Kevin B. Gregory, Lissa L. Webbon, Philippa H. Gander, J. Victor Lebacqz, "Alertness Management: Strategic Naps in Operational Settings," *Journal of Sleep Research* 4, supplement 2 (December 1995): 62–66.

15 Bhikkhu Nanamoli and Bhikkhu Bodhi, *The Middle Length Discourses of the Buddha* (Somerville, MA: Wisdom Publications, 1995), 342.

16 Bhikkhu Bodhi, *The Connected Discourses of the Buddha* (Somerville, MA: Wisdom Publications, 2000), 313.

17 Bhikkhu Bodhi, *The Numerical Discourses of the Buddha* (Somerville, MA: Wisdom Publications, 2012), 1573.

18 David S. Black, Gillian A O'Reilly, Richard E. Olmstead, Elizabeth C. Breen, and Michael R. Irwin, "Mindfulness Meditation and Improvement in Sleep Quality and Daytime Impairment among Older Adults with Sleep Disturbances," *JAMA Internal Medicine* 175, no. 4 (April 1, 2015): 494–501. doi: 10.1001/jamainternmed.2014.8081.

19 Sheila N. Garland, Eric S. Zhou, Brian D. Gonzalez, and Nicole Rodriguez, "The Quest for Mindful Sleep: A Critical Synthesis of the Impact of Mindfulness-Based Interventions for Insomnia," *Current Sleep Medicine Reports* 1, no. 3 (September 2016): 142–151. doi: 10.1007/s40675-016-0050-3.

CHAPTER 11: TELLING THE TRUTH

1 Thanissaro Bhikkhu, *The Buddhist Monastic Code I* (Valley Center, CA: Metta Forest Monastery, 2013), 291.

2 Moshe Walshe, *The Long Discourses of the Buddha* (Somerville, MA: Wisdom Publications, 1987), 462.

3 Bella M. DePaulo, Deborah A. Kashy, Susan E. Kirkendol, Melissa M. Wyer, and Jennifer A. Epstein, "Lying in Everyday Life," *Journal of Personality and Social Psychology* 70 (1996): 979. http://dx.doi.org/10.1037/0022-3514.70.5.979.

4 Keith Leavitt and David M. Sluss, "Lying for Who We Are: An Identity-Based Model of Workplace Dishonesty," *Academy of Management Review* 40, no. 4 (2005) https://doi.org/10.5465/amr.2013.0167.

5 Kim Scott, *Radical Candor* (New York: St. Martin's Press, 2017), 10.

6 Bhikkhu Bodhi, *The Buddha's Teachings on Social and Communal Harmony* (Somerville, MA: Wisdom Publications, 2016), 75.

7 Ibid., 81.

8 Ibid., 75.

9 Ibid., 60.

10 Scott, *Radical Candor*, 32.

11 Kate Crosby and Andrew Skilton, *The Bodhicaryavatra* (Oxford, UK: Oxford University Press, 1995), 41.

12 Bhikkhu, *Buddhist Monastic Code I*, 293.

13 Bhikkhu Nanamoli and Bhikkhu Bodhi, *The Middle Length Discourses of the Buddha* (Somerville, MA: Wisdom Publications, 1995), 524.

14 Gil Frondsal, *The Dhammapada* (Boulder, CO: Shamabhala Publications, 2005), 27.

CHAPTER 12: BICKERING BUDDHAS

1 Bhikkhu Bodhi, *The Numerical Discourses of the Buddha* (Somerville, MA: Wisdom Publications, 2012), 743.

2 Elfi Baillien, Jeroen Camps, Anja Vanden Broeck, Jeroen Stouten, LodeGodderis, Maarten Sercu, and Hans DeWitte "An Eye for an Eye Will Make the Whole World Blind: Conflict Escalation into Workplace Bullying and the Role of Distributive Conflict Behavior," *Journal of Business Ethics* 137, issue 2 (August 2016): 415–429. https://doi.org/10.1007/s10551-015-2563-y.

3 Bhikkhu Bodhi, *The Buddha's Teachings on Social and Communal Harmony* (Somerville, MA: Wisdom Publications, 2016), 76.

4 Ibid., 131.

CHAPTER 14: WHAT YODA GOT WRONG

1 Bhikkhu Bodhi, *The Connected Discourses of the Buddha* (Somerville, MA: Wisdom Publications, 2000), 1597.

2 Bhikkhu Bodhi, *The Noble Eightfold Path* (Onalaska, WA: Pariyatti Publishing, 2000), 63.

3 Moshe Walshe, *The Long Discourses of the Buddha* (Somerville, MA: Wisdom Publications, 1987), 462.

4 Tait D. Shanafelt, Colin P. West, Jeff A. Sloan, aul J. Novotny, Greg A. Poland, Ron Menaker, Teresa A. Rummans, and Lotte N. Dyrbye, "Career Fit and Burnout among Academic Faculty," *Archives of Internal Medicine* 169, no. 10 (2009: 990–995. doi:10.1001/archinternmed.2009.70.

5 Rita Gunther McGrath, "Failing by Design," *Harvard Business Review* 89, no. 4 (April 2011): 76–83, 137.

6 Daw Mya Tin, *The Dhammapada: Verses & Stories* (Delhi, India: Sri Satguru Publications, 1990), 380.

7 Gil Fronsdal, *The Dhammapada* (Boulder, CO: Shambhala Publications, 2005), 72. (I have translated tatagathas as "teachers," while Fronsdal leaves it untranslated.)

8 Matthew Bortolin, *The Dharma of Star Wars* (Somerville, MA: Wisdom Publications, 2015), xii.

CHAPTER 15: REMEMBERING TO BREATHE

1 Mark Twain, "The Late Benjamin Franklin," *The Galaxy* (July 1870): 138–140.

2 Kathleen Nolan, "Buddhism, Zen, and Bioethics," *Bioethics Yearbook* 3 (1993). https://doi.org/10.1007/978-94-011-1886-6_9.

3 Thich Nhat Hanh, *Breathe: You Are Alive!* (Berkeley, CA: Parallax Press, 2008), 3.

4   Eddie Stern, *One Simple Thing* (New York: North Point Press, 2019), 171.

5   Ibid., 145.

6   Thich Nhat Hanh's *Breathe: You Are Alive!* is especially good.

7   Bhikkhu Nanamoli and Bhikkhu Bodhi, *The Middle Length Discourses of the Buddha* (Somerville, MA: Wisdom Publications, 1995), 943.

CHAPTER 16: ATTACHMENT AND DETACHMENT

1   Oskar von Hinuber, *A Handbook of Pali Literature* (New Delhi, India: Munshiram Manoharlal Publishers, 1997), 24.

2   John D. Ireland, *Itivuttaka: The Buddha's Sayings* (Kandy, Sri Lanka: Buddhist Publication Society, 1997), 11.

3   Thomas Hugh Feeley, Jennie Hwang, and George A. Barnett, "Predicting Employee Turnover from Friendship Networks," *Journal of Applied Communication Research* 36, no. 1 (2008): 56–73. https://doi.org/10.1080/00909880701799790.

4   Charlotte Fritz, Chak Fu Lam, and Gretchen M. Spreitzer, "It's the Little Things That Matter: An Examination of Knowledge Workers' Energy Management," *Academy of Management Perspectives* 25, no. 3 (2017): 28–39. http://dx.doi.org/10.5465/AMP.2011.63886528

5   Rachel Morrison, "Gender Differences in the Relationship Between Workplace Friendships and Organisational Outcomes," *Enterprise and Innovation*, 2007, 33.

6   Julianna Pillemer and Nancy P. Rothbard, "Friends without Benefits: Understanding the Dark Sides of Workplace Friendship," *Academy of Management Review* 43, no. 4 (2018). https://doi.org/10.5465/amr.2016.0309.

7   Patricia M. Sias and Daniel J. Cahill, "From Coworkers to Friends: The Development of Peer Friendships in the Workplace," *Western Journal of Communication* 62, no. 3 (1998): 273–299. https://doi.org/10.1080/10570319809374611.

8   Fritz, et al., "It's the Little Things That Matter."

9   Charles A. Pierce and Herman Aguinis, "Bridging the Gap between Romantic Relationships and Sexual Harassment in Organizations," *Journal of Organizational Behavior* 18 (1997): 197–200.

10 Vanessa K. Bohns and Lauren A. DeVincent, "Rejecting Unwanted Romantic Advances Is More Difficult Than Suitors Realize," *Social Psychological and Personality Science* (2018): 1–9.

11 Ibid.

12 Bhikkhu Bodhi, *The Connected Discourses of the Buddha* (Somerville, MA: Wisdom Publications, 2000), 1524.

CHAPTER 17: BALANCING BETTER THAN BUDDHA

1   Mohan Wijyayaranta, *Buddhist Monastic Life: According to the Sources of the Theravada Tradition* (Cambridge, UK: Cambridge University Press, 1990), 173.

2   Bhikkhu Bodhi, *The Suttanipata* (Somerville, MA: Wisdom Publications, 2017), 223.

3   Erin Reid. "Embracing, Passing, Revealing, and the Ideal Worker Image: How People Navigate Expected and Experienced Professional Identities," *Organization Science* 26, no. 4 (2015): 997–1017. doi:10.1287/ORSC.2015.0975.

4   Charlotte Fritz, Chak Fu Lam, and Gretchen M. Spreitzer, "It's the Little Things That Matter: An Examination of Knowledge Workers' Energy Management," *Academy of Management Perspectives* 25, no. 3 (2017): 28–39. http://dx.doi.org/10.5465/AMP.2011.63886528

5   Evangelia Demerouti, Arnold B. Bakker, Sabine Sonnentag and Clive J. Fullagar "Work-Related Flow and Energy at Work and at Home: A Study on the Role of Daily Recovery," *Journal of Organizational Behavior* 33 (2012): 276–295. doi:10.1002/job.760.

6   Ellen Ernst Kossek and Brenda A. Lautsch, "Work-Life Flexibility for Whom? Occupational Status and Work-Life Inequality in Upper, Middle, and Lower Level Jobs," *Academy of Management Annals* 12, no. 1 (2017). .https://doi.org/10.5465/annals.2016.0059.

7   Bodhi, *The Suttanipata*, 742.

8   Hubert Nearman, O.B.C., translator, *The Monastic Office* (Mt. Shasta, CA: Shasta Abbey, 1993), 18.

CHAPTER 18: YOU ARE NOT YOUR JOB

1 Bhikkhu Bodhi, *The Connected Discourses of the Buddha* (Somerville, MA: Wisdom Publications, 2000), 901–903.

2 Rev. angel Kyodo williams, "Radical Challenge," in Rev. angel Kyodo williams, Lama Rod Owens, with Jasmine Syedullah, *Radical Dharma* (Berkeley, CA: North Atlantic Books, 2016), xxiii.

3 Zenju Earthlyn Manuel, *The Way of Tenderness: Awakening through Race, Sexuality, and Gender* (Somerville, MA: Wisdom Publications, 2015), 8.

CHAPTER 19: DEALING WITH DISTRACTIONS

1 Alex Soojung-Kim Pang, *The Distraction Addiction* (New York: Little, Brown and Company, 2013), 15.

2 Preetinder S. Gill, Ashwini Kamath, and Tejkaran S. Gill, "Distraction: An Assessment of Smartphone Usage in Health Care Work Settings," *Risk Management and Healthcare Policy* 5 (2012): 105–114. doi:10.2147/RMHP. S34813.

3 Ibid.

4 Jill T. Shelton, "The Distracting Effects of a Ringing Cell Phone: An Investigation of the Laboratory and the Classroom Setting," *Journal of Environmental Psychology* 29, no. 4 (December 2009): 513–521. doi:10.1016/j.jenvp.2009.03.001.

5 Bhikku Analayo, *Early Buddhist Meditation Studies* (Barre, MA: Barre Center for Buddhist Studies, 2017), 109.

6 Mihaly Csikszentmihalyi, Sami Abuhamdeh, and Jeanne Nakamura, "Flow," in Mihaly Csikszentmihalyi, *Flow and the Foundations of Positive Psychology* (Dordrecht, Germany: Springer, 2014), 230.

7 Shelton, "The Distracting Effects of a Ringing Cell Phone."

8 Wesley C. Clapp, Michael T. Rubens, Jasdeep Sabharwal, and Adam Gazzaley, "Deficit in Switching between Functional Brain Networks Underlies the Impact of Multitasking on Working Memory in Older Adults," *Proceeding of the National Academy of Science* 108, no. 17 (April 26, 2011): 7212–7217. doi: 10.1073/pnas.1015297108.

9 Faria Sana, TinaWeston, and Nicholas J.Cepeda, "Laptop Multitasking Hinders Classroom Learning for Both Users and Nearby Peers," Computers & Education 62 (March 2013): 24–31. https://doi.org/10.1016/j.compedu.2012.10.003.

10 Kate Crosby and Andrew Skilton, *The Bodhicaryavatra* (Oxford, UK: Oxford University Press, 1995), 36.

11 Alex Soojung-Kim Pang, *The Distraction Addiction* (New York: Little, Brown and Company, 2013), 61.

12 Ibid., 62.

13 Shunryu Suzuki, *Branching Streams Flow in the Darkness* (Berkeley: University of California Press, 1999), 3.

CHAPTER 20: BEGGING FOR LUNCH

1 Bhikkhu Nanamoli and Bhikkhu Bodhi, The Middle Length Discourses of the Buddha (Somerville, MA: Wisdom Publications, 1995), 134.

2 Malia Wollan, "Failure to Lunch: The Lamentable Rise of Desktop Dining," *New York Times Magazine* (February 27, 2016): 50.

3 Stephanie A. Boone and Charles P. Gerba, "The Prevalence of Human Parainfluenza Virus 1 on Indoor Office Fomites," *Food and Environmental Virology* 2 (2010): 41.

4 Stephanie A. Boone and Charles P. Gerba, "Significance of Fomites in the Spread of Respiratory and Enteric Viral Disease," *Applied and Environmental Microbiology* 73, no. 6 (March 2007): 1687–1696. doi:10.1128/AEM.02051-06. https://doi.org/10.1007/s12560-010-9026-5.

5 Thanaissaro Bhikkhu, *The Buddhist Monastic Code* (Valley Center, CA: Metta Forest Monastery, 2013), 497.

6 Evangelia Demerouti, Arnold B. Bakker, Sabine Sonnentag and Clive J. Fullagar "Work-Related Flow and Energy at Work and at Home: A Study on the Role of Daily Recovery," *Journal of Organizational Behavior* 33 (2012): 276– 295. doi: 10.1002/job.760.

7 Jessica de Bloom, Ulla Kinnunen, and Kalevi Korpela, "Exposure to Nature versus Relaxation during Lunch Breaks and Recovery from Work: Development and Design of an

Intervention Study to Improve Workers' Health, Well-Being, Work Performance and Creativity," *BMC Public Health* 14 (2014): 488. doi: 10.1186/1471-2458-14-488.

8 Bhikkhu Bodhi, *The Connected Discourses of the Buddha* (Somerville, MA: Wisdom Publications, 2000), 176.

9 Bhikkhu Anālayo, "Overeating and Mindfulness in Ancient India," *Mindfulness* 9 (2018): 1648–1654. https://doi.org/10.1007/s12671-018-1009-x.

10 See the chapter titled "Food for Thought, Thought for Food," in Tara Cottrell and Dan Zigmond, *Buddha's Diet* (Philadelphia: Running Press, 2016).

11 Michael T. French, Johanna Catherine Maclean, Jody L. Sindelar, and Hai Fang, "The Morning After: Alcohol Misuse and Employment Problems," *Applied Economics* 43, no. 21 (2011):, 2705–2720. https://doi.org/10.1080/00036840903357421.

12 Silje L. Kaspersen, Kristine Pape,Gunnhild Å. Vie,Solveig O. Ose, Steinar Krokstad, David Gunnell, and Johan H. Bjørngaard, "Health and Unemployment: 14 Years of Follow-Up on Job Loss in the Norwegian HUNT Study," *European Journal of Public Health* 26, no. 2 (April 2016): 312–317. https://doi.org/10.1093/eurpub/ckv224.

13 Rupert Gethin, *Sayings of the Buddha: A Selection of Suttas from the Pali Nikāyas* (Oxford, UK: Oxford University Press, 2008), 131.

CHAPTER 21: WHO WOULD BUDDHA FIRE?

1 Bureau of Labor Statistics, US Department of Labor, "Labor Force Statistics from the Current Population Survey" (January 19, 2018). https://www.bls.gov/cps/cpsaat11.htm.

2 Gil Fronsdal, *The Dhammapada* (Boulder, CO: Shambhala Publications, 2005), 1.

3 Thanissaro Bhikkhu, *The Buddhist Monastic Code I* (Valley Center, CA: Metta Forest Monastery, 2013), 329.

4 Bhikkhu Bodhi, *The Numerical Discourses of the Buddha* (Somerville, MA: Wisdom Publications, 2012), 816.

5 Damien P. Horigan, "Of Compassion and Capital Punishment: A Buddhist Perspective on the Death Penalty," *American Journal of Jurisprudence* 41 (1996). http://ccbs.ntu.edu.tw/FULLTEXT/JR-PIIII/damin2.htm; Leanne Fiftal Alarid and Hsiao-Ming Wang, "Mercy and Punishment: Buddhism and the Death Penalty," *Social Justice* 28, no. 1 (2001): 231–247. http://www.jstor.org/stable/29768067.

6 Fronsdal, Dhammapada, 13.

CHAPTER 22: WALKING AWAY

1 Steven D. Levitt, "Heads or Tails: The Impact of a Coin Toss and Major Life Decisions and Subsequent Happiness," *National Bureau of Economic Research*, Working Paper 22587 (August 2016). http://www.nber.org/papers/w22487.

2 Ibid., 16.

3 Wendy R. Boswell, John W. Boudreau, Jan Tichy, "The Relationship between Employee Job Change and Job Satisfaction: The Honeymoon-Hangover Effect," *Journal of Applied Psychology* 90, no. 5 (September 2005): 882–892.

4 Moshe Walshe, *The Long Discourses of the Buddha* (Somerville, MA: Wisdom Publications, 1987), 482.

5 Bhikkhu Bodhi, *The Numerical Discourses of the Buddha* (Somerville, MA: Wisdom Publications, 2012), 790.

6 Walshe, *Long Discourses of the Buddha*, 69–70.

7 Bhikkhu Bodhi, *The Connected Discourses of the Buddha* (Somerville, MA: Wisdom Publications, 2000), 1333.

8 Bureau of Labor Statistics, U.S. Department of Labor, "Number of Jobs, Labor Market Experience, and Earnings Growth among Americans at 50: Results from a Longitudinal Survey" (August 24, 2017). https://www.bls.gov/news.

9 Gil Fronsdal, The Dhammapada (Boulder, CO: Shambhala Publications, 2005), 14.

CHAPTER 23: DATA-DRIVEN DHARMA

1 Bhikkhu Nanamoli, *The Life of the Buddha* (Onalska, WA: BPS Pariyatti Editions, 2001), 17–18.

2 Ibid.

3 Bhikkhu Bodhi, *The Numerical Discourses of the Buddha* (Somerville, MA: Wisdom Publications, 2012), 285.

4 Bhikkhu Nanamoli and Bhikkhu Bodhi, *The Middle Length Discourses of the Buddha* (Somerville, MA: Wisdom Publications, 1995), 780.

CHAPTER 24: LIVING IN THE PRESENT MOMENT

1 Thich Nhat Hanh, *Present Moment, Wonderful Moment* (Berkeley, CA: Parallax Press, 1990), vii.

2 Ibid., viii.

CHAPTER 25: SERVING ALL SENTIENT BEINGS

1 Larry Yang, *Awakening Together* (Boston: Wisdom Publications, 2017), 41–42.

2 His Holiness the 14th Dalai Lama, *Kindness, Clarity, and Insight* (Boston: Snow Lion, 1984).

3 Dan Zigmond, "A Toast to Paying Attention!" *Lion's Roar* (January 2019).

4 Stephen Batchelor, *A Guide to the Bodhisattva Way of Life* (Dharamsala, India: Library of Tibetan Works and Archives, 1999).

5 Kate Crosby and Andrew Skilton, *The Bodhicaryavatra* (Oxford, UK: Oxford University Press, 1995), 43.

CHAPTER 26: DID YOU JUST BECOME A BUDDHIST?

1 Robert Wright, *Why Buddhism Is True* (New York: Simon & Schuster, 2017).

2 Ibid., 261.

3 Bhikkhu Nanamoli and Bhikkhu Bodhi, *The Middle Length Discourses of the Buddha* (Somerville, MA: Wisdom Publications, 1995), 484.

Index

Fulfillment, xvii, 5–7, 98, 113. *See also* Job satisfaction

G

Gambling, 97
Gender, 58, 112–114, 129, 143
Germs, 136–137
Goals, achieving, 4–6, 88–95, 101, 150–153
Great Awakening, xiii–xiv, 18–24, 28, 93–94, 96–97, 157, 166–167. *See also* Awakening
"Guide to the Bodhisattva Way of Life," 170

H

Hanh, Thich Nhat, *See* Thich Nhat Hanh
Happiness
benefits of, 10–11
finding, xvii, 122–123, 156–160, 174
productivity and, 10–11
Harassment, 114
Health, improving, 54–55, 58–71, 112, 174
Heart disease, 58–59, 67
Helping others, 166–170
Hiring workers, 142
Honesty, 72–78, 146, 160, 174
How to Meditate, 177
Huffington, Arianna, 67

I

Identity, 124–129
Idleness, 57, 89, 97, 101

Illnesses, 136–137
"Imposter's syndrome," 47–48
Incompetence, feelings of, 47–48, 74, 127
Insomnia, 67–68, 71. *See also* Sleep
Internet browsing, 54–55, 133
Intoxicants, xv–xvi, 150
Itivuttaka, 110–111

J

Job, changing, 149–153
Job, quitting, 3–7, 149–153
Job satisfaction, 5–7, 67–68, 98, 113, 150–153. *See also* Work
Jogging, 64–65

K

Karma, 48, 143–147, 172
Khujjuttara, 110–111
Kindness, 76, 146–147, 174

L

Laziness, 7, 66, 97
Levitt, Steve, 148–149, 152
Lies, telling, 72–78
Life
balance in, 7, 22–24, 97–99, 116–123, 133–134, 174
drifting through, xv, 18
half-lived life, 18
present moments in, 162–165
Lifelong learning, 123
Life-work balance, 7, 97–99, 116–123, 133–134, 174